HE WHO GETS SLAPPED

He Who Gets Slapped

A PLAY IN FOUR ACTS

By LEONID ANDREYEV

TRANSLATED FROM THE RUSSIAN
WITH AN INTRODUCTION BY

GREGORY ZILBOORG

COPYRIGHT, 1922, BY BRENTANO'S
COPYRIGHT, 1921, BY THE DIAL PUBLISHING CO.
COPYRIGHT, (IN RENEWAL) 1949, BY GREGORY ZILBOORG

All Rights Reserved

CAUTION : — Professionals and amateurs are hereby warned that "HE WHO GETS SLAPPED," being fully protected under the copyright laws of the United States of America, the British Empire, including the Dominion of Canada, and other countries of the Copyright Union, is subject to a royalty, and anyone presenting the play without the consent of the author or his authorized agents will be liable to the penalties by law provided. The amateur acting rights are available only in limited territory. Do not make any arrangement for the presentation of this play without first securing permission and terms in writing from Samuel French, 25 West 45th Street, New York, N. Y.

NEW YORK
SAMUEL FRENCH
PUBLISHER
25 WEST 45TH STREET

LONDON
SAMUEL FRENCH, LTD.
26 SOUTHAMPTON ST.,
STRAND, W.C.2

Theodore Lownik Library
St. Procopius College
Lisle, Illinois

891.7
A55hE
1949

HE WHO GETS SLAPPED

All Rights Reserved

Especial notice should be taken that the possession of this book without a valid contract for production first having been obtained from the publisher, confers no right or license to professionals or amateurs to produce the play publicly or in private for gain or charity.

In its present form this play is dedicated to the reading public only, and no performance, representation, production, recitation, public reading, or radio broadcasting may be given except by special arrangement with Samuel French, 25 West 45th Street, New York.

On application to Samuel French, 25 West 45th Street, New York, N. Y., royalty will be quoted for amateur use in those cities and towns where the play is not restricted.

Whenever the play is produced the following notice must appear on all programs, printing and advertising for the play: "Produced by special arrangement with Samuel French of New York."

Attention is called to the penalty provided by law for any infringement of the author's rights, as follows:

"SECTION 4966:—Any person publicly performing or representing any dramatic or musical composition for which copyright has been obtained, without the consent of the proprietor of said dramatic or musical composition, or his heirs and assigns, shall be liable for damages thereof, such damages, in all cases to be assessed at such sum, not less than one hundred dollars for the first and fifty dollars for every subsequent performance, as to the court shall appear to be just. If the unlawful performance and representation be wilful and for profit, such person or persons shall be guilty of a misdemeanor, and upon conviction shall be imprisoned for a period not exceeding one year."—U. S. Revised Statutes: Title 60, Chap. 3.

The first regular production of HE in English was by The Theatre Guild on January 9, 1922, at the Garrick Theatre, New York. The original cast was as follows:

Tilly } Polly } *Musical Clowns*	{ Philip Leigh { Edgar Stehli
Briquet, Manager of the Circus	Ernest Cossart
Mancini, Consuelo's Father	Frank Reicher
Zinida, a Lion Tamer	Helen Westley
Angelica } Estelle } *Trapeze Performers* . . .	{ Martha Bryan Allen { Helen Sheridan
Francois	. Edwin R. Wolfe
HE	Richard Bennett
Jackson, a Clown	Henry Travers
Consuelo, the Equestrian Tango Queen . . .	Margalo Gillmore
Alfred Bezano, a Bareback Rider	John Rutherford
Baron Regnard	. Louis Calvert
A Gentleman	. John Blair
Wardrobe Lady	. Kathryn Wilson
Usher	Charles Cheltenham
Conductor	. Edwin R. Wolfe
Pierre	. Philip Loeb
A Sword Dancer	. Renee Wilde
Ballet Master	. Oliver Grymes
Ballet Girls . . . . {	Vera Tompkins Anne Tonnetti Marguerite Wernimont Frances Ryan
Actresses in Circus Pantomime	{ Adele St. Maur { Sara Enright
Thomas, a Strong Man	. Dante Voltaire
A Snake Charmer	. Joan Clement
A Contortionist	Richard Coolidge
A Riding Master	. Kenneth Lawton
A Juggler	Francis G. Sadtler
Acrobats	{ Sears Taylor { Luigi Belastro

Stage Manager, Philip Loeb *Ass't Stage Manager*, Oliver Grymes

Produced under the direction of ROBERT MILTON

Settings and Costumes by LEE SIMONSON

v

CAST OF CHARACTERS

CONSUELO—*a bareback rider in a circus. Billed as "The Bareback Tango Queen."*

MANCINI—*Consuelo's father.*

HE—*a clown in Briquet's circus. Billed as "HE Who Gets Slapped."*

BRIQUET—*Manager of the circus.*

ZINIDA—*a lion tamer, Briquet's wife*

ALFRED BEZANO—*a bareback rider*

A GENTLEMAN.

BARON REGNARD.

JACKSON—*a clown.*

TILLY ⎫
POLLY ⎬ *—musical clowns.*

THOMAS, ANGELICA, *and other actors and actresses of Briquet's circus.*

The action takes place in one of the large cities of France.

INTRODUCTION

Leonid Andreyev as a literary figure was born in the gloomy atmosphere of depression of the 'nineties. He thus appeared upon the literary stage at a period when the old and splendid generation of Turgenev and Dostoevsky had already passed away and when Chekhov had begun to demonstrate before the reader the gloom and colourlessness of Russia life.

This was a period when the social forces of Russia were half destroyed by the reaction under Alexander III, and when the young generation was trying to rest and to get away from the strain of social hopes and despair. This period, briefly speaking, was a period of melancholy, of commonplace, every-day preoccupations, and of dull *terre à terre* philosophy.

It must be borne in mind that literature was the only outlet for the moral and intellectual forces of Russia. Political reaction, censorship, complete absence of civil liberties, and the cult of popular ignorance upon which Czardom based its power, all these made the written artistic word almost the sole expression of Russian social longings and idealistic expectations.

It is therefore only natural that Russian literature in its general development is closely interwoven with the political and social conditions of Russia at the given moment. The 'nineties were a period of depression. After the assassination of Alexander II (1881) and the subsequent tightening of the chain of reaction, combined with a general *débâcle* in progressive and radical circles, the Russian intellectual fell into a state of pessimism. His faith in an early liberation was shattered, his hope of recovery was broken. Chekhov is the most characteristic representative of that period; he himself called his heroes "the dull-grey people."

Maxim Gorki and Leonid Andreyev appeared almost simultaneously at that time. The former brought the message of a rebel spirit which forecast a new moral upheaval, a new social protest; the latter appeared clad in the gloom of his time, which he strangely combined with a spirit of almost anarchistic revolt. From the point of view of historical completeness Leonid Andreyev is more representative of the epoch, demonstrating at once two contradictory elements of the Russia of the 'nineties: lack or even absence of faith interwoven with protest and mutiny.

Andreyev is symbolic and romantic. Her Majesty Fate and His Excellency Accident, these are the two dark, unknown, at times brutal forces which dwelt ever before the mind's eye. His symbols are full of horror and at times unbending atrocity. Beginning with his short stories, In Fog, The Life of Basil of Thebes, through his dramas, The Life of Man, and Anathema, until his last writings, he saw human beings in the form of ghosts and ghosts in the form of human beings dominating every step, every breath of life. Still his gruesome symbolism, despite his genius for rendering his images in a clear-cut, almost crystalline manner, did not appeal to many of his contemporaries because the dark shroud in which Andreyev enveloped life was impenetrable and at times it was impossible to discern in that gloom the few values which Andreyev still found in life. Leo Tolstoy said once: "Leonid Andreyev tries to frighten me, but I am not afraid."

Even in his splendid realistic dramas it is difficult for Andreyev to rid himself of the habit of symbolizing and dimming the few rays of light which try to filter through.

There was nevertheless a little corner in Andreyev's artistic heart where there appeared some indefinite hope which never acquired a specific artistic form, but which was alluded to many times in his writings. In his short story, Thought, he makes fragmentary allusions to his half-hope, half-idea: "If the lot of the Man be to become a God, his throne will be the Book," says the hero.

But the red laugh of the Russo-Japanese war, the

abortive revolution of 1905, the general ignorance
and darkness of the masses, the strain of the last war,
the depreciation of human life as a value in itself,
brought Leonid Andreyev to the last step of the
pessimistic ladder which he was ever descending into
the abyss of hopelessness. This state of mind is best
illustrated by his last dramatic work, HE, the One
Who Gets Slapped.

Here we see a man of high education, of great intellectual achievement, who leaves life, willingly in
appearance, but forcibly in fact. The relations of
man to man, of group to group, according to Andreyev are such that the Man is forced to efface himself. Even Thought, or the Book, could not help the
Man to become a God. He becomes a clown. He
performs stunts, he gets slaps; the public laughs, being
unaware that this laughter is a mockery at itself, at
its culture, at its thought, at its achievement.

The characters of the play, as the reader will see,
are depicted with a bitter sarcasm and unfriendliness,
for Andreyev seems to have lost his last faith in the
Man. The good, the innocent and clean heart is
bound to suffer and die. His Consuelo, Zinida, Bezano are only stray rays of light out of place in the
world and even in the world-circus which is full of
spiders, champagne, and human outcasts. Andreyev
does not blame these outcasts. On the contrary, he
feels sympathy, if for anybody, for just these clowns,

jugglers, and bareback-riders; but life, this strange combination of fate, accident, and cowardly slander, is stronger, and they collapse under the burden of this combination.

HE is perhaps the best work of Andreyev, at any rate his best dramatic work. It is more adapted to stage conditions than his previous plays and is not overcrowded with symbolic ghosts. Furthermore, HE is a remarkable summary of Andreyev's philosophy.

GREGORY ZILBOORG

HE WHO GETS SLAPPED

HE WHO GETS SLAPPED

ACT I

A very large, rather dirty room, with whitewashed walls. To the left, in a niche, is a window, the only out-side window in the room, opening on a court-yard. The light from it is so dim that even by day the elec-tricity has to be turned on.

At the very top of the centre-back wall is a row of small dusty windows. They open on the circus hall. At night, when the performance is going on, a bright light shines through. By day they are dark. In the same wall is a large white door, reached by two stone steps, and nailed fast.

On the right, almost in the corner, is a high, wide, arched doorway which leads to the stables and the ring. By day it opens into pale darkness, at night into pale light.

The room is used for many purposes. It is the office of Papa Briquet, manager of the circus; here he keeps his little desk. It is the cloak-room of some of the actors. It is also the room where the cast gathers be-tween calls, during rehearsals or performances. Again, it is a check-room for used circus property, such as gilt

*armchairs, scenery for pantomimes, and other wares of
the circus household. The walls are covered with circus
announcements and glaring posters.*

*The time is morning. In the circus hall a rehearsal
is going on, and preparations are being made for the
evening performance. As the curtain goes up, the
cracking whip and the shouts of the riding-master are
heard from the ring. The stage is empty for a few
seconds, then enter Tilly and Polly, the musical clowns,
practising a new march. Playing on tiny pipes, they
step from the dark doorway to the window. Their
music is agreeable to the ear, but small, mincing, arti-
ficially clown-like, like their mincing steps; they wear
jackets and resemble each other; same smooth-shaven
face, same height; Tilly, the younger, has a scarf
around his neck; both have their derbies on the backs
of their heads. Tilly glances through the window, then
they turn about, still marching.*

POLLY

[*Interrupting the march*]: Stop, you're out again!
Now, listen—[*He stands close to Tilly and plays into
his face. Tilly absent-mindedly listens, scratching his
nose.*] There! Come on now! [*They resume their
music and marching. As they reach the door they meet
the manager and* MANCINI; *the latter walks behind the
manager, and is gnawing at the knob of his gold-*

*mounted cane. COUNT MANCINI is tall and slight. The
seams of his clothes are worn and he keeps his coat but-
toned tight. He assumes extremely graceful manners,
takes affected poses, and has a special fondness for
toying with his cane, with aristocratic stylishness.
When he laughs, which happens often, his thin sharp
face takes on a marked resemblance to a satyr. The
manager, "PAPA" BRIQUET, is a stout quiet man of
average height. His bearing is hesitant. The clowns
make room for the gentlemen. The manager looks
questioningly at the older man.]*

POLLY

[*With an affected accent*]: Our moosic for the pan-
tomime! The March of the Ants!

BRIQUET

Ha! Yes!
[*The gentlemen walk in. The clowns resume their
     music, POLLY marching on, then turning, the
     younger following.*]

POLLY

Papa Briquet, Jack is working very badly to-day.

BRIQUET

What's the matter with him?

POLLY

He has a sore throat. You'd better take a look at him.

BRIQUET

All right. Come on, Jack. Open your mouth! Wider—wider. [*Turns clown's face to the light near the window and examines him closely and seriously.*] Just smear it with iodine.

POLLY

I told him so. I said it was nothing! Oh! Come on. [*They go away playing, marching, practising their funny mincing steps. The manager sits down.* MANCINI *strikes a pose by the wall, smiling ironically.*]

MANCINI

So. You give them medical treatment, too! Look out, Papa Briquet, you have no licence.

BRIQUET

Just a little advice. They're all so afraid for their lives.

MANCINI

His throat is simply burnt with whiskey. These

two fellows get drunk every night. I am amazed, Papa Briquet, to see you pay so little attention to their morals. [*He laughs.*]

BRIQUET

You make me sick, Mancini.

MANCINI

Count Mancini is at your service!

BRIQUET

You make me sick, Count Mancini. You poke your nose into everything, you disturb the artists in their work. Some day you'll get a thrashing, and I warn you that I shan't interfere.

MANCINI

As a man of superior associations and education I cannot be expected to treat your actors as my equals! What more can you ask, Briquet? You see that I do you the honour of speaking with you quite familiarly, quite simply.

BRIQUET

Ha! ha! ha! [*Slightly threatening*] Really!—

Mancini

Never mind my joke. What if they did dare attack
me—ever seen this, Briquet? [*He draws a stiletto
out of his cane and advances it silently.*] Useful little
thing. By the way, you have no idea of the discovery
I made yesterday in a suburb. Such a girl! [*Laughs.*]
Oh, well! all right, all right—I know you don't like
that sort of sport. But look here, you must give me
a hundred francs!

Briquet

Not a sou.

Mancini

Then I'll take away Consuelo—that's all——

Briquet

Your daily threat!

Mancini

Yes, my threat! And you would do the same, if
you were as shamefully hard up as I am. Now look
here, you know as well as I do that I have to live up
to my name somehow, keep up the family reputation.
Just because the tide of ill-fortune which struck my
ancestors compelled me to make my daughter, the

Countess Veronica, a bareback rider—to keep us from
starving—do you understand—you heartless idiot!

Briquet

You chase the girls too much! Some day you'll
land in jail, Mancini!

Mancini

In jail? Oh, no! Why, I have to uphold our
name, the splendour of my family, [*laughs*] haven't
I? The Mancinis are known all over Italy for their
love of girls—just girls! Is it my fault if I must
pay such crazy prices for what my ancestors got free
of charge? You're nothing but an ass, a *parvenu*
ass. How can you understand Family Traditions? I
don't drink—I stopped playing cards after that accident—no, you need not smile. Now if I give up the
girls, what will be left of Mancini? Only a coat of
arms, that's all—— In the name of family traditions, give me a hundred francs!

Briquet

I told you no, I won't.

Mancini

You know that I leave half of the salary for Con-

suelo—but—perhaps you think I do not love my child
—my only daughter, all that remains to me as a
memory of her sainted mother—what cruelty! [*Pre-
tends to cry, wipes his eyes with a small and dirty
lace handkerchief, embroidered with a coronet.*]

BRIQUET

Why don't you say, rather, that she is foolish
enough to give you half her salary. You make me
sick——

[*Enter Zinida, the lion tamer; burningly beautiful,
her self-confident, commanding gestures at first
glance give an impression of languor. She is
BRIQUET'S unmarried wife.*]

ZINIDA

[*To* MANCINI]: Good morning.

MANCINI

Madame Zinida! This barbarian, this brute may
pierce me with his dagger, but I cannot control the
expression of my love! [*Kneels facetiously before her*]
Madame! Count Mancini has the honour of asking
you to be his wife. . . .

ZINIDA

[*To* BRIQUET]: Money?

BRIQUET

Yes.

ZINIDA

Don't give him any. [*Sits down wearily on a torn sofa, shuts her eyes.* MANCINI *gets up and wipes his knees.*]

MANCINI

Duchess! Don't be cruel. I am no lion, no tiger, no savage beast which you are accustomed to tame. I am merely a poor domestic animal, who wants, miaow, miaow, a little green grass.

ZINIDA

[*Without opening her eyes*]: Jim tells me you have a teacher for Consuelo. What for?

MANCINI

The solicitude of a father, duchess, the solicitude and the tireless anxiety of a loving heart. The extreme misfortunes of our family, when I was a child, have left some flaws in her education. Friends, the daughter of Count Mancini, Countess Veronica, can barely read! Is that admissible? And you, Briquet, heartless brute, you still ask why I need money!

Zinida

Artful!

Briquet

What are you teaching her?

Mancini

Everything. A student had been giving her lessons, but I threw him out yesterday. He had the nerve to fall in love with Consuelo and stood there miaowing at the door like a cat. Everything, Briquet, that you don't know—literature, mythology, orthography——
[*Two young actresses appear, with small fur coats thrown over their light dresses. They are tired and sit down in the corner.*]

Mancini

I do not wish my daughter——

Zinida

Artful!

Briquet

You are stupid, Mancini. What do you do it for? [*In a didactic tone*] You are fearfully stupid, Mancini. Why does she need to learn? Since she is here she need never know anything about that life. Don't you understand? What is geography? If I were the government I would forbid artists to read books. Let them read the posters, that's enough.

[*During* BRIQUET'S *speech, the two clowns and another actor enter. They sit down wearily.*]

BRIQUET

Right now, your Consuelo is an excellent artist, but just as soon as you teach her mythology, and she begins to read, she'll become a nuisance, she'll be corrupted, and then she'll go and poison herself. I know those books, I've read 'em myself. All they teach is corruption, and how to kill oneself.

FIRST ACTRESS

I love the novels that come out in the newspaper.

BRIQUET

That shows what a foolish girl you are. You'll be done for in no time. Believe me, my friends, we must forget entirely what is happening out there. How can we understand all that goes on there?

MANCINI

You are an enemy of enlightenment, you are an obscurantist, Briquet.

Briquet

And you are stupid. You are from out there. What has it taught you? [*The actors laugh.*] If you'd been born in a circus as I was, you'd *know* something. Enlightenment is plain nonsense—nothing else. Ask Zinida. She knows everything they teach out there—geography, mythology—— Does it make her any happier? You tell them, dear.

Zinida

Leave me alone, Louis.

Mancini

[*Angrily*]: Oh! Go to the devil! When I listen to your asinine philosophy, I'd like to skin you for more than a paltry hundred francs—for two hundred —for a thousand. Great God! What an ass of a manager! Yes, right before every one of them I want to say that you are a stingy old skinflint—that you pay starvation wages. I'll make you give Consuelo a raise of a hundred francs. Listen, all you honest vagabonds, tell me—who is it draws the crowd that fills the circus every night? You? a couple of musical donkeys? Tigers, lions? Nobody cares for those hungry cats!

Zinida

Leave the tigers alone.

MANCINI

Beg your pardon, Zinida. I did not mean to hurt your feelings—honestly. I really marvel at your furious audacity—at your grace—you are a heroine —I kiss your tiny hands. But what do they understand about heroism? [*An orchestra softly plays the Tango in the circus. He continues with enthusiasm.*] Hear! hear! Now tell me, honest vagabonds, who but Consuelo and Bezano draws the crowds! That Tango on horseback—it is—it is—— Oh, the devil! Even his fatuousness the Pope could not withstand its lure.

POLLY

True! It's a great trick—wasn't the idea Bezano's?

MANCINI

Idea! Idea! The lad's in love, like a cat—that's the idea. What's the good of an idea without a woman! You wouldn't dance very far with your idea alone, eh, Papa Briquet?

BRIQUET

We have a contract.

MANCINI

Such base formalities.

Zinida

Give him ten francs and let him go.

Mancini

Ten! Never! *Fifteen!* Don't be stubborn, Papa
For the traditions of my house—twenty. I swear—
on my honour—I can't do with less. [Briquet *hands
him   twenty francs. Nonchalantly*) *Merci.* Thanks.

Zinida

Why don't you take it from your baron?

Mancini

[*Raising his eyebrows haughtily, quite indignant*]:
From the Baron? Woman! who do you think I am
that I should be beholden to a stranger?

Zinida

You're plotting something artful. I know you very
little, but I guess you're an awful scoundrel.

Mancini

[*Laughs*]: Such an insult from such beautiful lips.
[*Enter an "artist," apparently an athlete.*]

ATHLETE

Papa Briquet, there's a gentleman from beyond the grave asking for you.

ACTRESS

A ghost?

ATHLETE

No. He seems alive. Did you ever see a drunken ghost?

BRIQUET

If he's drunk, tell him I'm out, Thomas. Does he want to see me or the Count?

ATHLETE

No, you. Maybe he's not drunk, but just a ghost.

MANCINI

[*Draws himself together, puffs up*]: A society man?

ATHLETE

Yes. I'll tell him to come in.

[*One hears the whip cracking in the ring. The Tango*

*sounds very low and distant—then comes nearer
—louder.   Silence.*]

BRIQUET

[*Touching* ZINIDA's *arm*]:   Tired?

ZINIDA

[*Drawing back a little*]:   No.

POLLY

Your red lion is nervous to-day, Zinida!

ZINIDA

You shouldn't tease him.

POLLY

I played a melody from Traviata for him.   And he
sang with me.   Wouldn't that be a good trick to
stage, Papa Briquet?

[THOMAS *brings in the gentleman, points out the
manager, and goes heavily away.   The gentleman is not young, and he is ugly, but his rather
strange face is bold and lively.   He wears an expensive overcoat, with a fur collar, and holds his
hat and gloves in his hand.*]

GENTLEMAN

[*Bowing and smiling*] : Have I the pleasure of addressing the manager?

BRIQUET

Yes. Won't you sit down, please? Tilly, bring a chair.

GENTLEMAN

Oh! Don't trouble. [*Looks around.*] These are your artists? Very glad——

MANCINI

[*Straightening and bowing slightly*] : Count Mancini.

GENTLEMAN

[*Surprised*] : Count?

BRIQUET

[*Indignantly*] : Yes, Count. And whom have I the honour of——

GENTLEMAN

I don't quite know myself—yet. As a rule you

choose your own names, don't you? I have not chosen
yet. Later you might advise me about it. I have an
idea already, but I am afraid it sounds too much like
literature—you know.

BRIQUET

Literature?

GENTLEMAN

Yes! Too sophisticated. [*They all look surprised.*]
I presume these two gentlemen are clowns? I am so
glad. May I shake hands with them? [*Stands up
and shakes hands with clowns, who make silly faces.*]

BRIQUET

Excuse me—but what can I do for you?

GENTLEMAN

[*With the same pleasant, confident smile*]: Oh.
You do something for me? No. I want to do something for you, Papa Briquet.

BRIQUET

Papa Briquet? But you don't look like——

GENTLEMAN

[*Reassuringly*]: It's all right. I shall become
"like." These two gentlemen just made remarkable

faces. Would you like to see me imitate them? Look!
[*He makes the same silly faces as the clowns.*]

BRIQUET

Yes! [*Involuntarily*] You are not drunk, sir?

GENTLEMAN

No. I don't drink as a rule. Do I look drunk?

POLLY

A little.

GENTLEMAN

No—I don't drink. It is a peculiarity of my talent.

BRIQUET

[*Familiarly*]: Where did you work before? Juggler?

GENTLEMAN

No. But I am glad you feel in me a comrade, Papa Briquet. Unfortunately I am not a juggler, and have worked nowhere—I am—just so.

MANCINI

But you look like a society man.

GENTLEMAN

Oh, you flatter me, Count. I am just so.

BRIQUET

Well, what do you want? You see I am obliged to tell you that everything is taken.

GENTLEMAN

That's immaterial. I want to be a clown, if you will allow me. [*Some of the actors smile*, BRIQUET *begins to grow angry.*]

BRIQUET

But what can you do? You're asking too much. What can you do?

GENTLEMAN

Why! Nothing! Isn't that funny! I can't do a thing.

BRIQUET

No, it's not funny. Any scoundrel knows that much.

GENTLEMAN

[*Rather helpless, but still smiling and looking around*]: We can invent something——

BRIQUET

[*Ironically*] : From literature?

[*The clown Jackson enters slowly without being no-*
ticed by the others. He stands behind the gen-
tlemen.]

GENTLEMAN

Yes, one can find something literary, too. A nice
little speech for instance on, let's say, a religious
topic. Something like a debate among the clowns.

BRIQUET

A debate! The devil! This is no academy.

GENTLEMAN

[*Sadly*] : I am very sorry. Something else then.
Perhaps a joke about the creation of the world and its
rulers?

BRIQUET

What about the police? No, no—nothing like
that!

JACKSON

[*Coming forward*] : The rulers of the world? You
don't like them? I don't either. Shake.

BRIQUET

[*Introducing*]: Our chief clown, the famous Jackson.

GENTLEMAN

[*Enthusiastically*]: Great heavens—you! Allow me to shake hands with you heartily! You, with your genius, you have given me so much joy!

JACKSON

I'm glad indeed!

BRIQUET

[*Shrugs his shoulders; to Jackson*]: He wants to be a clown! Look him over, Jim.
[*Jackson makes a motion at which the gentleman hurriedly removes his coat and throws it on a chair. He is ready for the examination. Jackson turns him round, looking him over critically.*]

JACKSON

Clown? Hm! Turn round then. Clown? Yes? Now smile. Wider—broader—do you call that a smile? So—that's better. There is something, yes— but for full developments—— [*Sadly*] Probably you can't even turn a somersault?

GENTLEMAN

[*Sighs*]: No.

JACKSON

How old are you?

GENTLEMAN

Thirty-nine. Too late? [*Jackson moves away with a whistle. There is a silence.*]

ZINIDA

[*Softly*]: Take him.

BRIQUET

[*Indignant*]: What the hell shall I do with him if he doesn't know a thing? He's drunk!

GENTLEMAN

Honestly I am not. Thank you for your support, Madame. Are you not the famous Zinida, the lion tamer, whose regal beauty and audacity——

ZINIDA

Yes. But I do not like flattery.

Gentleman

It is not flattery.

Mancini

You are evidently not accustomed to good society, my dear. Flattery? This gentleman expresses his admiration in sincere and beautiful words—and you—you are not educated, Zinida. As for myself——
[*Enter* Consuelo *and* Bezano *in circus costume.*]

Consuelo

You here, Daddy?

Mancini

Yes, my child, you are not tired? [*Kisses her on the forehead.*] My daughter, sir, Countess Veronica. Known on the stage as Consuelo, The Bareback Tango Queen. Did you ever see her?

Gentleman

I have enjoyed her work. It is marvellous!

Mancini

Yes! Of course. Everyone admits it. And how do you like the name, Consuelo? I took it from the novel of George Sand. It means "Consolation."

GENTLEMAN

What a wonderful knowledge of books!

MANCINI

A small thing. Despite your strange intention, I can see, sir, that you are a gentleman. My peer! Let me explain to you, that only the strange and fatal misfortunes of our ancient family—"*sic transit gloria mundi*," sir.

CONSUELO

It's a bore, Daddy—— Where's my handkerchief, Alfred?

BEZANO

Here it is.

CONSUELO

[*Showing the handkerchief to the gentleman*]: Genuine Venetian. Do you like it?

GENTLEMAN

[*Again bowing*]: My eyes are dazzled, how beautiful! Papa Briquet, the more I look around me the more I want to stay with you. [*Makes the face of a simpleton.*] On the one hand a count, on the other——

JACKSON

[*Nods approval*]: That's not bad. Look here, think a bit—find something. Everyone here thinks for himself.

[*Silence. The gentleman stands with a finger on his forehead, thinking.*]

GENTLEMAN

Find something—find something . . . Eureka!

POLLY

That means *found*. Come!

GENTLEMAN

Eureka—— I shall be among you, he who gets slapped. [*General laughter. Even* BRIQUET *smiles.*]

GENTLEMAN

[*Looks at them smiling*]: You see I made even you laugh—is that easy? [*All grow serious. Polly sighs.*]

TILLY

No, it's not easy. Did you laugh, Polly?

POLLY

Sure, a lot. Did you?

TILLY

I did. [*Imitating an instrument, he plays with his lips a melody at once sad and gay.*]

JACKSON

"He Who Gets Slapped," that's not bad.

GENTLEMAN

It's not, is it? I rather like it myself. It suits my talent. And comrades, I have even found a name— you'll call me "HE." Is that all right?

JACKSON

[*Thinking*]: "HE"—Not bad.

CONSUELO

[*In a singing, melodic voice*]: "HE" is so funny— "HE"—like a dog. Daddy, are there such dogs? [*Jackson suddenly gives a circus slap to the gentleman. HE steps back and grows pale.*]

GENTLEMAN

What!—[*General laughter covers his exclamation.*]

JACKSON

HE Who Gets Slapped. Or didn't you get it?

Polly

[*Comically*]: He says he wants more——
[*The gentleman smiles, rubbing his cheek.*]

Gentleman

So sudden.—Without waiting.—How funny—you
didn't hurt me, and yet my cheek burns.

[*Again there is loud laughter. The clowns cackle like
    ducks, hens, cocks; they bark. Zinida says some-
    thing to Briquet, casts a glance toward Bezano,
    and goes out. Mancini assumes a bored air and
    looks at his watch. The two actresses go out.*]

Jackson

Take him, Papa Briquet—he will push us.

Mancini

[*Again looking at his watch*]: But bear in mind,
that Papa Briquet is as close as Harpagon. If you
expect to get good money here you are mistaken.
[*HE laughs.*] A slap? What's a slap? Worth only
small change, a franc and a half a dozen. Better go
back to society; you will make more money there.
Why for one slap, just a light tap, you might say,
my friend, Marquis Justi, was paid fifty thousand
lire!

BRIQUET

Shut up, Mancini. Will you take care of him, Jackson.

JACKSON

I can.

POLLY

Do you like music? A Beethoven sonata played on a broom, for instance, or Mozart on a bottle?

HE

Alas! No. But I will be exceedingly grateful if you will teach me. A clown! My childhood's dream. When all my school friends were thrilled by Plutarch's heroes, or the light of science—I dreamed of clowns. Beethoven on a broom, Mozart on bottles! Just what I have sought all my life! Friends, I must have a costume!

JACKSON

I see you don't know much! A costume [*putting his finger on his forehead*] is a thing which calls for deep thought. Have you seen my Sun here? [*Strikes his posterior.*] I looked for it two years.

He

[*Enthusiastically*]: I shall think!

Mancini

It is time for me to go. Consuelo, my child, you
must get dressed. [*To HE.*] We are lunching with
Baron Regnard, a friend of mine, a banker.

Consuelo

But I don't want to go, Daddy. Alfred says I
must rehearse to-day.

Mancini

[*Horrified, holding up his hands*]: Child, think of
me, and what a situation you put me in! I promised
the Baron, the Baron expects us. Why, it is impossible! Oh, I am in a cold sweat.

Consuelo

Alfred says——

Bezano

[*Drily*]: She has to work. Are you rested? Then
come on.

MANCINI

But—the devil take me if I know what to make of it. Hey, Bezano, bareback rider! Are you crazy? I gave you permission for Art's sake, to exercise my daughter's talent—and you——

CONSUELO

Go along, Papa, and don't be so silly. We've got to work, haven't we? Have lunch along with your Baron. And Daddy, you forgot to take a clean handkerchief again, and I washed two for you yesterday. Where did you put them?

MANCINI

[*Ashamed, blushing*]: Why, my linen is washed by the laundress, and you, Consuelo, are still playing with toys. It is stupid! You're a chatter-box. You don't think. These gentlemen might imagine Heaven knows what. How stupid. I'm off.

CONSUELO

Do you want me to write him a little note?

MANCINI

[*Angrily*]: A little note? Your little notes would make a horse laugh! Good-bye.
[*He goes out toying angrily with his cane. The*

clowns follow him respectfully, playing a funeral march. HE and Jackson *laugh. The actors disappear one by one.*]

Consuelo

[*Laughing*]: Do I really write so badly? And I love so to write. Did you like my note, Alfred—or did you laugh, too?

Bezano

[*Blushing*]: No, I did not. Come on, Consuelo. [*They go, and meet* Zinida, *entering. Consuelo passes on.*]

Zinida

Are you going back to work, Bezano?

Bezano

[*Politely*]: Yes. To-day is a very bad day. How are your lions, Zinida? I think the weather affects them.

Consuelo

[*From the ring*]: Alfred!

ZINIDA

Yes. Some one is calling you. You'd better go. [*Alfred goes out. To* BRIQUET] Are you finished?

BRIQUET

Right away.

JACKSON

Then good-bye till evening. Think about your costume, HE, and I shall look for some idea, too. Be here at ten to-morrow. Don't be late, or you'll get another slap. And I'll work with you.

HE

I shall not be late. [*He looks after* JACKSON *who goes out.*] Must be a nice man. All the people about you are so nice, Papa Briquet. I suppose that good-looking bareback rider is in love with Consuelo, isn't he? [*Laughs.*]

ZINIDA

It's none of your business. For a newcomer you go poking your nose too far. How much does he want, Papa?

BRIQUET

Just a minute. See here HE. I don't want to make a contract with you.

HE

Just as you please. Do you know what? Don't let us talk about money. You are an honest fellow, Briquet; you will see what my work is worth to you, and then——

BRIQUET

[*Pleased*]: Now that's very nice of you. Zinida, the man really doesn't know anything.

ZINIDA

Well, do as he suggests. Now we must write it down. Where's the book?

BRIQUET

Here. [*To HE.*] I don't like to write [*gives book to* ZINIDA), but we have to put down the names of the actors, you know—it's police regulations. Then if anyone kills himself, or——

[*Again comes the sound of the Tango, and calls from the ring.*]

ZINIDA

What is your name?

HE

[*Smiling*]: HE. I chose it, you know. Or don't you like it?

BRIQUET

We like it all right—but we have to have your real name. Have you a passport?

HE

[*Confused*]: A passport? No, I have none. Or, rather, yes. I have something of the kind, but I had no idea the rules were strictly enforced here. What do you need papers for?
[ZINIDA *and* BRIQUET *look at each other.* ZINIDA *pushes the book aside.*]

ZINIDA

Then we can't take you. We cannot quarrel with the police, just on your account.

BRIQUET

She is my wife. I hadn't told you. She's right. You might get hurt by a horse, or hurt yourself—or

do something. We don't know you, you see. I per-
sonally don't care, but out there, it's different, you
see. For me a corpse is just a corpse—and I don't
ask anything about him. It's up to God or the Devil.
But they—they're too curious. Well, I suppose it's
necessary for order. I don't know—— Got a card?

HE

[*Rubs his head, thinking*]: What shall I do? I
have my card, but [*smiles*] you understand that I
don't want my name to be known.

BRIQUET

Some story, hey?

HE

Yes, something like that. Why can't you imagine
that I have no name? Can't I lose it as I might lose
my hat? Or let someone else take it by mistake?
When a stray dog comes to you, you don't ask his
name—you simply give him another. Let me be that
dog. [*Laughing*] HE—the Dog!

ZINIDA

Why don't you tell us your name, just the two of
us. Nobody else need know it. Unless you should
break your neck——

HE

[*Hesitates*]: Honestly?   [ZINIDA *shrugs her shoulders.*]

BRIQUET

Where people are honest, their word is good.   One sees you come from *out there*.

HE

All right.   But please, don't be surprised.   [*Gives* ZINIDA *his card.   She looks at it, then hands it to* BRIQUET, *then both look at HE.*]

BRIQUET

If it is true, sir, that you are really what is written here——

HE

For heaven's sake—for heaven's sake—this does not exist, but was lost long ago; it is just a check for an old hat.   I pray you to forget it, as I have.   I am HE Who Gets Slapped—nothing else.   [*Silence.*]

BRIQUET

I beg your pardon, sir, but I must ask you again, I must humbly ask you—are you not drunk, sir? There is something in your eye—something——

HE

No, no. I am He, Who Gets Slapped. Since when do you speak to me like this, Papa Briquet? You offend me.

ZINIDA

After all, it's his business, Briquet. [*She hides the card.*] Truly you are a strange man. [*Smiles.*] And you have already noticed that Bezano is in love with the horse-girl? And that I love my Briquet, did you notice that, too?

HE

[*Also smiling*]: Oh, yes. You adore him.

ZINIDA

I adore him. Now go with him, Briquet, show him the ring and the stables—I have something to write.

HE

Yes, yes, please. I am so happy. At last you have taken me, haven't you? It is true—you're not joking. The circus, the tan-bark, the ring in which I shall run getting my slaps. Yes, yes, Briquet, let's go. Until I feel the sawdust under my feet, I shall not believe it.

BRIQUET

All right then. [*Kisses* ZINIDA.] Come on.

ZINIDA

Just a minute—HE! Answer me a question. I have a man who takes care of the cages, a plain fellow whom nobody knows. He just cleans the cages you know; he walks in and out whenever he wants to, without even looking at the lions, as if he were perfectly at home. Why is that so? Nobody knows him, everybody knows me, everyone is afraid for me, while—— And he is such a silly man—you will see him. [*Laughs.*] But don't you think of entering the cage yourself! My red one would give you such a slap!

BRIQUET

[*Displeased*]: There you are again, Zinida— stop it.

ZINIDA

[*Laughs*]: All right—go. Oh yes, Louis, send me Bezano. I have to settle an account with him.

[*HE and the director go out. ZINIDA looks at the card once more, then hides it. She gets up and walks quickly up and down the room. She stops*

to listen to the Tango, which ends abruptly.
Then she stands motionless, looking straight at
the dark opening of the door through which
BEZANO *comes.*]

BEZANO

[*Entering*]: You called me, Zinida? What do
you want? Tell me quickly, I have no time——
[ZINIDA *looks at him silently.* BEZANO *flushes with*
anger, and knits his eyebrows. He turns to the
door to go.]

ZINIDA

Bezano!

BEZANO

[*Stops, without looking up*]: What do you want?
I have no time.

ZINIDA

Bezano! I keep hearing people say that you are in
love with Consuelo. Is it true?

BEZANO

[*Shrugging his shoulders*]: We work well together.

ZINIDA

[*Takes a step forward*]: No—— Tell me, Alfred, do you love her?

BEZANO

[*Flushes like a boy, but looks straight into* ZINIDA's *eyes. Proudly*]: I do not love anybody. No, I love nobody. How can I? Consuelo? She is here to-day, gone to-morrow, if her father should take her away. And I? Who am I? An acrobat, the son of a Milanese shoemaker—— She! I cannot even talk about it. Like my horses I have no words. Who am I to love?

ZINIDA

Do you love me? A little?

BEZANO

No. I told you before.

ZINIDA

Still no? Not even a little?

BEZANO

[*After a silence*]: I am afraid of you.

ZINIDA

[*Wants to cry out, indignantly, but masters herself and lowers her eyes, as if in an effort to shut out their light; turns pale*]: Am I . . . so terrifying a woman——

BEZANO

You are beautiful, like a queen. You are almost as beautiful as Consuelo. But I don't like your eyes. Your eyes command me to love you—and I don't like to be commanded. I am afraid of you.

ZINIDA

Do I command, Bezano? No—only implore.

BEZANO

Then why not look at me straight? Now I have it. You know yourself that your eyes cannot implore. [*Laughs.*] Your lions have spoiled you.

ZINIDA

My red lion loves me——

BEZANO

Never! If he loves you, why is he so sad?

ZINIDA

Yesterday he was licking my hands like a dog.

BEZANO

And this morning he was looking for you to devour you. He thrusts out his muzzle and looks out, as if he sees only you. He is afraid of you, and he hates you. Or do you want me to lick your hands too, like a dog?

ZINIDA

No, Alfred, but I—I want to kiss *your* hand. [*With passion*]: Give it to me!

BEZANO

[*Severely*]: I am ashamed to listen to you when you speak like that.

ZINIDA

[*Controlling herself*]: One should not torture another as you torture me. Alfred, I love you. No, I do not command. Look into my eyes—— *I love you.* [*Silence.*]

BEZANO

[*Turns to go*]: Good-bye.

ZINIDA

Alfred——

[*HE appears in the doorway, and stops.*]

BEZANO

Please never tell me any more that you love me. I don't want it. Otherwise I will quit. You pronounce the word love as if you were cracking me with your whip. You know it is disgusting——

[*He turns brusquely and goes. Both notice HE; BEZANO, frowning, passes out quickly. ZINIDA returns to her place at the desk, with a proudly indifferent expression.*]

HE

[*Coming in*]: I beg your pardon, but I——

ZINIDA

There you are again, poking your nose into everything, HE. Do you really want a slap?

HE

[*Laughing*]: No. I simply forgot my overcoat. I didn't hear anything.

ZINIDA

I don't care whether you did or not.

HE

May I take my coat?

ZINIDA

Take it if it's yours. Sit down, HE.

HE

I am sitting down.

ZINIDA

Now tell me HE, could you love me?

HE

[*Laughing*]: I? I and Love! Look at me, Zinida.
Did you ever see a lover with such a face?

ZINIDA

One can succeed with such a face——

HE

That's because I am happy—because I lost my hat
—because I am drunk—or perhaps I am not drunk.

But I feel as dizzy as a young girl at her first ball.
It is so nice here—slap me, I want to play my part.
Perhaps it will awaken love in my heart, too. Love—
[*as if listening to his own heart with pretended ter-
ror*] do you know—I feel it!
[*In the circus the Tango is played again.*]

ZINIDA

[*Listening too*]: For me?

HE

No. I don't know. For everyone. [*Listens to the
music.*] Yes, they are dancing—how beautiful Consuelo is—and how beautiful is the youth. He has the
body of a Greek God; he looks as if he had been
modeled by Praxiteles. Love! Love! [*Silence,
music.*]

ZINIDA

Tell me, HE——

HE

At your service, Queen!

ZINIDA

HE, what shall I do, to make my lions love me?

CURTAIN

ACT II

The same room, during the evening performance. Occasional music, laughter, shrieks, and applause are audible. Through the small windows, back centre, the light is shining.

Consuelo and Baron Regnard occupy the stage; Consuelo wears her stage costume; she sits with her feet on the sofa, a small shawl covering her shoulders. Before her stands the Baron, a tall stout man in evening dress, a rose in his buttonhole; grasping the ground with feet well apart, he gazes at her with convex spider-like eyes.

Baron

Is it true that your father, the Count, has introduced you to a certain Marquis Justi, a very rich man?

Consuelo

[*Surprised*]: No, he is only joking. I have often heard him speak of a Marquis Justi but I have never seen him——

Baron

And do you know that your father is just a charlatan?

49

CONSUELO

Oh! Don't say that—Father is such a dear.

BARON

Did you like the jewels?

CONSUELO

Yes, very much. I was very sorry when Father told me I must return them. He said it would not be nice for me to keep them. I even cried a little about it.

BARON

Your father is only a beggar and a charlatan.

CONSUELO

Oh, no, don't scold him—he loves you so much.

BARON

Let me kiss your hand——

CONSUELO

Oh, no, it isn't proper! One may kiss the hand only when one says how do you do or good-bye. But in the meantime you can't.

BARON

Everybody is in love with you, that is why you and your father make such a fuss about yourselves. Who is that new clown they call HE? I don't like him, he's too shrewd a beast. . . . Is he in love with you, too? I noticed the way he looked at you. . . .

CONSUELO

[*Laughing*]: Nothing of the kind. He is so funny! He got fifty-two slaps yesterday. We counted them. Think of it, fifty-two slaps! Father said, "if they had only been gold pieces."

BARON

And Bezano, Consuelo. . . . Do you like him?

CONSUELO

Yes, very much. He is so good-looking. He says that Bezano and I are the most beautiful couple in the world. HE calls him Adam, and me Eve. But that's improper, isn't it? HE is *so* improper.

BARON

And does HE speak to you very often?

Consuelo

Yes, often. . . . But I don't understand him.
It seems as if he were drunk.

Baron

"Consuelo"! . . . It means in Spanish . . .
Consolation. Your father is an ass. . . . Consuelo, I love you.

Consuelo

Talk it over with Father.

Baron

[*Angry*]: Your father is a swindler and a charlatan. He should be turned over to the police. **Don't**
you understand that I *cannot* marry you?

Consuelo

But Father says you can. . . .

Baron

No, I cannot. And what if I shoot myself? Consuelo, silly girl, I love you unbearably . . . unbearably, do you understand? I am probably mad
. . . and must be taken to a doctor, yanked about,

beaten with sticks. Why do I love you so much,
Consuelo?

CONSUELO

Then, you'd better marry.

BARON

I have had a hundred women, beauties, but I didn't
see them. You are the first and I don't see any one
else. Who strikes man with love, God or the Devil?
The Devil struck me. Let me kiss your hand.

CONSUELO

No. [*She thinks a while and sighs.*]

BARON

Do you think sometimes? What are you thinking
about now Consuelo?

CONSUELO

[*With another sigh*]: I don't know why, I just
felt sorry for Bezano. [*Sighs again.*] He is so nice
to me when he teaches me . . . and he has such
a tiny little room.

BARON

[*Indignant*]: You were there?

Consuelo

No. He told me about it. [*Smiling*] Do you hear the noise in there? That's He getting slapped. Poor thing . . . although I know it doesn't hurt, it's only make-believe. The intermission is coming soon.

[*The* Baron *throws away his cigar, takes two quick steps forward, and falls on his knees before the girl.*]

Baron

Consuelo——

Consuelo

Please, don't. Get up. Please leave my hand alone.

Baron

Consuelo!

Consuelo

[*Disgusted*]: Get up please, it's disgusting—you're so fat.

[*The* Baron *gets up. Voices are heard near the door and in the ring. It is the intermission. The clowns come first, talking cheerfully and excitedly. HE leads them, in his clown's dress, with*

*painted eyebrows and white nose; the others are
applauding him. Voices of the actors calling:
"Bravo! HE." Then come the actors and actresses, riding-masters, and the rest, all in costume. ZINIDA is not among them. PAPA BRI-
QUET comes a little later.]*

POLLY

A hundred slaps! Bravo, HE!

JACKSON

Not bad, not bad at all. You'll make a career.

TILLY

He was the Professor to-day, and we were the stu-
dents. Here goes another! [*Gives him a clown's
slap. Laughter. All bid good evening to the* BARON.
*He is politely rude to these vagabonds who bore him,
and remains silent. They seem quite used to it. Enter*
MANCINI. *He is the same, and with the same cane.*]

MANCINI

[*Shaking hands*]: What a success, Baron—and
think of it—how the crowd does love slaps. [*Whispering*] Your knees are dusty, Baron, brush them
off. The floor is very dirty in here. [*Aloud*] Con-

suelo, dear child, how do you feel? [*Goes over to his daughter.   Sound of laughing, chattering.   The waiters from the buffet in the lobby bring in soda and wine.   Consuelo's voice is heard.*]

CONSUELO

And where is Bezano?

HE

[*Bows before the* BARON, *affecting intimacy*] : *You* do not recognize me, Baron?

BARON

Yes I do.   You are the clown, HE.

HE

Yes I am HE Who Gets Slapped.   May I presume to ask you, Baron, did you get your jewels back?

BARON

What!

HE

I was asked to return some jewels to you, and I take the liberty of—— [*The* BARON *turns his back on him—HE laughs loudly.*]

JACKSON

Whiskey and soda! Believe me, ladies and gents,
HE will surely make a career. I am an old clown, and
I know the crowd. Why to-day, he even eclipsed *me*
—and clouds have covered my Sun. [*Striking it.*]
They do not like puzzles, they want slaps! They are
longing for them and dreaming about them in their
homes. Your health, HE! Another whiskey and
soda! HE got so many slaps to-day, there would be
enough to go round the whole orchestra!

TILLY

I bet there wouldn't! [*To Jackson*] Shake!

POLLY

I bet there wouldn't—I'll go and count the old
mugs.

A VOICE

The orchestra did not laugh——

JACKSON

Because they were getting it, but the galleries did,
because they were looking at the orchestra getting
slapped. Your health, HE!

He

Your's Jim! Tell me, why didn't you let me finish my speech—I was just getting a good start.

Jackson

[*Seriously*]: My friend, because your speech was a sacrilege. Politics—all right. Manners—as much as you want. But Providence—leave it in peace. And believe me, friend, I shut your mouth in time. Didn't I, Papa Briquet?

Briquet

[*Coming nearer*]: Yes. It was too much like literature. This is not an academy. You forget yourself, He.

Tilly

But to shut one's mouth—faugh. . . .

Briquet

[*In a didactic tone* : Whenever one shuts one's mouth, it is always high time to shut it, unless one is drinking. Hey, whiskey and soda!

Voices

Whiskey and soda for the Manager!

Mancini

But this is obscurantism. Philosophizing again, Briquet?

Briquet

I am not satisfied with you to-day, He. Why do you tease them? They don't like it. Your health! A good slap must be clean like a crystal—fft-fft! right side, left side, and done with it. They will like it; they will laugh, and love you. But in your slaps there is a certain bite, you understand, a certain smell——

He

But they laughed, nevertheless!

Briquet

But without pleasure, without pleasure, He. You pay, and immediately draw a draft on their bank; it's not the right game—they won't like you.

Jackson

That's what *I* tell him. He had already begun to make them angry.

Bezano

[*Entering*]: Consuelo, where are you? I have been looking for you—come on. [*Both go out. The*

BARON, *after hesitating a while, follows them.* MAN-
CINI *accompanies him respectfully to the door.*]

HE

[*Sighs*]: You don't understand, my dear friends;
you are simply old, and have forgotten the smell of
the stage.

JACKSON

Aha! Who is old, my young man?

HE

Don't be angry, Jim. It's a play, don't you understand? I become happy when I enter the ring and
hear the music. I wear a mask and I feel humorous.
There is a mask on my face, and I play. I may say
anything like a drunkard. Do you understand? Yesterday when I, with this stupid face, was playing the
great man, the philosopher [*he assumes a proud mon-
umental pose, and repeats the gesture of the play—
general laughter*] I was walking this way, and was
telling how great, how wise, how incomparable I was
—how God lived in me, how high I stood above the
earth—how glory shone above my head [*his voice
changes and he is speaking faster*] then you, Jim,
you hit me for the first time. And I asked you,
"What is it, they're applauding me?" Then, at the

tenth slap, I said: "It seems to me that they sent
for me from the Academy?" [*Acts, looking around
him with an air of unconquerable pride and splendour.
Laughter. Jackson gives him a real slap.*]

HE

[*Holding his face*]: Why?

JACKSON

Because you're a fool, and play for nothing.
Waiter, the check. (*Laughter. The bell calls them
to the ring. The actors go out in haste, some running. The waiters collect their money.*)

BRIQUET

[*In a sing-song*]: To the ring—to the ring—

MANCINI

I want to tell you something, HE. You are not
going yet?

HE

No. I'll take a rest.

BRIQUET

To the ring—to the ring—
[*The clowns as they go sing in shrill, squeaky voices,
    Little by little they all disappear, and loud*

*music begins. HE seats himself on the sofa with
his legs crossed, and yawns.*]

MANCINI

HE, you have something none of my ancestors ever
had—money. Let's have a nice bottle on you. Waiter,
please—[*The waiter who was taking up dishes, brings
a bottle of wine and glasses and goes out.*]

HE

You're blue, Mancini. [*Stretches.*] Well, at my
age, a hundred slaps—it seems pretty hard. So
you're blue. How are things getting on with your
girl?

MANCINI

Tss!   Bad!   Complications—parents—[*shudders*]
Agh—

HE

Prison!

MANCINI

[*Laughing*]: Prison! Mustn't I uphold the glory
of my name now, eh? HE, I'm joking—but there is
Hell in my heart. You're the only one who under-

stands me. But tell me how to explain this passion? It will turn my hair grey, it'll bring me to prison, to the grave. I am a tragic man. HE—[*Wipes his eyes with a dirty handkerchief.*] Why don't I like things which are not forbidden? Why, at all moments, even at the very moment of ecstasy, must I be reminded of some law—it is stupid. HE, I am becoming an anarchist. Good God!—Count Mancini, an anarchist. That's the only thing I've missed.

HE

Isn't there a way of settling it somehow?

MANCINI

Is there a way of getting money, somehow?

HE

And the Baron?

MANCINI

Oh, yes! He's just waiting for it, the bloodsucker! He'll get what he's after. Some day, you'll see me give him Consuelo for ten thousand francs, perhaps for five!

HE

Cheap.

Mancini

Did I say it was anything else? Do I want to do it? But these bourgeois are strangling me, they've got me by the throat. He, one can easily see that you're a gentleman, and of good society, you understand me—I showed you the jewels which I sent back to him—damn honesty—I didn't even dare change the stones, put false ones—

He

Why?

Mancini

It would have queered the game. Do you think he didn't weigh the diamonds when he got them back?

He

He will not marry her.

Mancini

Yes he will. You don't understand. [*Laughs.*] The first half of his life, this man had only appetites—now love's got him. If he does not get Consuelo, he is lost, he is—like a withered narcissus. Plague take him with his automobiles. Did you see his car?

HE

I did. . . . Give Consuelo to the Jockey—

MANCINI

To Bezano? [*Laughs.*] What nonsense you do talk! Oh, I know. It's your joke about Adam and Eve. But please stop it. It's clever, but it compromises the child. She told me about it.

HE

Or give her to me.

MANCINI

Have you a billion? [*Laughs.*] Ah, HE, I'm not in the proper mood to listen to your clownish jokes— They say there are terrible jails in this country, and no discriminations are being made between people of my kind, and plain scoundrels. Why do you look at me like that? You're making fun of me?

HE

No.

MANCINI

I'll never get accustomed to those faces. You'ı ª so disgustingly made up.

HE

He will not marry her. You can be as proud as
you please, Mancini, but he'll not marry her. What
is Consuelo? She is not educated. When she is off
her horse, any good housemaid from a decent house
has nicer manners, and speaks better. [*Nonchalantly*] Don't *you* think she's stupid?

MANCINI

No, she's not stupid. And you, HE, are a fool.
What need has a woman of intelligence? Why, HE,
you astonish me. Consuelo is an unpolished jewel,
and only a real donkey does not notice her sparkle.
Do you know what happened? I tried to begin to
polish her—

HE

Yes, you took a teacher. And what happened?

MANCINI

[*Nodding his head*]: I was frightened—it went
too fast—I had to dismiss him. Another month or
two, and *she* would have kicked *me* out. [*Laughs.*]
The clever old diamond merchants of Amsterdam keep
their precious stones unpolished, and fool the thieves.
My father taught me that.

He

The sleep of a diamond. It is only sleeping, then. You are wise, Mancini.

Mancini

Do you know what blood flows in the veins of an Italian woman? The blood of Hannibal and Corsini—of a Borgia—and of a dirty Lombardi peasant—and of a Moor. Oh! an Italian woman is not of a lower race, with only peasants and gypsies behind her. All possibilities, all forms are included in her, as in our marvelous sculpture. Do you understand that, you fool? Strike here—out springs a washerwoman, or a cheap street girl whom you want to throw out, because she is sloppy and has a screechy voice. Strike there—but carefully and gently, for there stands a queen, a goddess, the Venus of the Capitol, who sings like a Stradivarius and makes you cry, idiot! An Italian woman—

He

You're quite a poet, Mancini! But what will the Baron make of her?

Mancini

What? What? Make of *her?* A baroness, you fool! What are you laughing at? I don't get you?

But I am happy that this lovesick beast is neither a
duke nor a prince—or she would be a princess and
I—what would become of me? A year after the wed-
ding they would not let me even into the kitchen
[*laughing*] not even into the kitchen! I, Count
Mancini, and she a—a simple—

HE

[*Jumping up*]: What did you say? You are not
her father, Mancini?

MANCINI

Tss—the devil—I am so nervous to-day! Heavens,
who do you think I am? "Her father?" Of course
[*tries to laugh*] how silly you are—haven't you noticed the family resemblance? Just look, the nose,
the eyes— [*Suddenly sighs deeply.*] Ah, HE! How
unhappy I am! Think of it. Here I am, a gentleman, nearly beaten in my struggle to keep up the
honour of my name, of an old house, while there in
the parquet—there sits that beast, an elephant with
the eyes of a spider . . . and he looks at Consuelo
. . . and . . .

HE

Yes, yes, he has the motionless stare of a spider—
you're right!

MANCINI

Just what I say—a spider! But I must, I shall compel him to marry her. You'll see— [*Walking excitedly up and down, playing with his cane.*] You'll see! All my life I've been getting ready for this battle. [*He continues to walk up and down. Silence. Outside, great stillness.*]

HE

[*Listening*]: Why is it so quiet out there? What a strange silence.

MANCINI

[*Disgusted*]: I don't know. Out there it is quiet—but here [*touching his forehead with his cane*] here is storm, whirlwind. [*Bends over the clown.*] HE, shall I tell you a strange thing—an unusual trick of nature? [*Laughs, and looks very important.*] For three centuries the Counts Mancini have had no children! [*Laughs.*]

HE

Then how were you born?

MANCINI

Sh! Silence! That is the secret of our sainted mothers! Ha-ha! We are too ancient a stock—too exquisitely refined to trouble ourselves with such things—matters in which a peasant is more competent than ourselves. [*Enter an usher.*] What do you want? The manager is on the stage.

THE USHER

Yes, sir. Baron Regnard wished me to give you this letter.

MANCINI

The Baron? Is he there?

THE USHER

Baron Regnard has left. There is no answer.

MANCINI

[*Opening the envelope, his hand shaking*]: The devil—the devil! [*The usher is going.*]

HE

Just a minute. Why is there no music? This silence . . .

THE USHER

It is the act with Madame Zinida and her lions. [*He goes.* MANCINI *is reading the* BARON'S *note for the second time.*]

HE

What's the matter, Mancini? You shine like Jackson's sun.

MANCINI

What's the matter, did you ask? What's the matter? What's the matter? [*Balancing his cane, he takes steps like a ballet-dancer.*]

HE

Mancini! [MANCINI *rolls his eyes, makes faces dances.*] Speak, you beast!

MANCINI

[*Holds out his hand*]: Give me ten francs! Quick —ten francs—here, come on. [*Puts it automatically into his vest pocket.* Listen, HE! If in a month I don't have a car of my own, you may give me one of your slaps!

HE

What! He's going to marry? He's decided?

MANCINI

What do you mean by "decided?" [*Laughs.*] When a man has the rope about his neck, you don't ask him about his health! Baron—[*Stops suddenly, startled.* BRIQUET *is staggering in like a drunken man, his hand over his eyes.*]

HE

[*Goes to him, touches his shoulder gently*]: What is the matter, Papa Briquet? Tell me!

BRIQUET

[*Groaning*]: Oh, oh, I can't . . . I can't . . . Ah—

HE

Something has happened? You are ill? Please speak.

BRIQUET

I can't look at it! [*Takes his hands from his eyes, opens them wide.*] Why does she do it? Ah, ah, why does she do it? She must be taken away; she is insane. I couldn't look at it. [*Shivers.*] They will tear her to pieces. HE—her lions—they will tear her—

MANCINI

Go on, Briquet. She is always like that. You act like a child. You ought to be ashamed.

BRIQUET

No— To-day she is mad! And what is the matter with the crowd? They are all like dead people— they're not even breathing. I couldn't stand it. Listen—what's that? [*All listen. There is the same silence.*]

MANCINI

[*Disturbed*]: I'll go and see.

BRIQUET

[*Yelling*]: No! Don't! You can't look—damned profession! Don't go. You will scorch her—every pair of eyes that looks at her—at her lions—no, no. It is impossible—it is a sacrilege. I ran away. . . . HE, they will tear her——

HE

[*Tries to be cheerful*]: Keep cool, Papa Briquet— I had no idea you were such a coward. You ought to be ashamed. Have a drink. Mancini, give him some wine.

BRIQUET

I don't want any. Heavens, if it were only over— [*All listen.*] I have seen many things in my

life, but this . . . Oh, she is crazy. [*All still listen.
Suddenly the silence breaks, like a huge stone wall
crashing. There is a thunder of appause, mixed with
shouts, music, wild screams—half bestial, half human.
The men give way, relieved. Briquet sinks to a seat.*]

MANCINI

[*Nervous*]: You see—you see—you old fool!

BRIQUET

[*Sobs and laughs*]: I am not going to allow it
any more!

HE

Here she is!
[*Zinida walks in, alone. She looks like a drunken
bacchante, or like a mad woman. Her hair falls
over her shoulders dishevelled, one shoulder is un-
covered. She walks unseeing, though her eyes
glow. She is like the living statue of a mad
Victory. Behind her comes an actor, very pale,
then two clowns, and a little later Consuelo and
Bezano. All look at Zinida fearfully, as if they
were afraid of a touch of her hand, or her great
eyes.*]

BRIQUET

[*Shouting*]: You are crazy—you're a mad woman!

ZINIDA

I? No. Did you see? Did you see? Well? [*She stands smiling, with the expression of a mad Victory.*]

TILLY

[*Plaintively*]: Cut it out, Zinida. Go to the devil!

ZINIDA

You saw, too! And! . . . what—

BRIQUET

Come home—come home. [*To the others*] You can do what you like here. Zinida, come home.

POLLY

You can't go, Papa. There's still your number.

ZINIDA

[*Her eyes meet those of Bezano*]: Ah! Bezano. [*Laughs long and happily.*] Bezano! Alfred! Did you see? My lions *do* love me! [*Bezano, without answering, leaves the stage. Zinida seems to wither and grow dim, as a light being extinguished. Her smile fades, her eyes and face grow pale. Briquet anxiously bends over her.*]

BRIQUET

[*In a slow voice*]: A chair! [*Zinida sits. Her head drops on her shoulder, her arms fall, she begins to shiver and tremble. Some one calls, "Cognac"— an actor runs to get it.*]

BRIQUET

[*Helpless*]: What is the matter, Zinida darling?

MANCINI

[*Running about*]: She must quiet down. Get out, get out—vagabonds! I'll fix everything, Papa Briquet. The wrap—where's the wrap? She's cold. [*A clown hands it to him; they cover her.*]

TILLY

[*Timidly*]: Wouldn't you like some moosic?

MANCINI

[*Giving her some cognac*]: Drink, Duchess, drink! Drink it all—that's it. [ZINIDA *drinks it like water, evidently not noticing the taste. She shivers. The clowns disappear one by one.* CONSUELO, *with a sudden flexible movement, falls on her knees before* ZINIDA *and kisses her hands, warming them between her own.*]

CONSUELO

Dear, dear, you are cold! Poor little hands, dear good one, beloved one——

ZINIDA

[*Pushes her away, gently*]: Ho—home. It will soon be over. It's nothing . . . I am ver—very . . . home. . . . You stay here, Briquet— you must. I'm all right.

CONSUELO

You are cold? Here is my shawl.

ZINIDA

No—let me. . . . [CONSUELO *gets up, and moves aside.*]

BRIQUET

And it's all because of your books, Zinida—your mythology. Now tell me, why do you want those beasts to love you? Beasts! Do you understand, HE? You too, you're from that world. She'll listen more to you. Explain it to her. Whom can those beasts love? Those hairy monsters, with diabolic eyes?

He

[*Genially*]: I believe—only their equals. You are right, Papa Briquet—there must be the same race.

Briquet

Of course, and this is all nonsense—literature. Explain it to her, He.

He

[*Takes on a meditative air*]: Yes, you are right, Briquet.

Briquet

You see, dear, silly woman—everybody agrees. . . .

Mancini

Oh! Briquet, you make me sick; you are an absolute despot, an Asiatic.

Zinida

[*With the shadow of a smile, gives her hand to be kissed*]: Calm yourself, Louis. It is over—I am going home. [*She stands up, shaking, still chilled.*]

Briquet

But how? alone, dear?

Mancini

What! fool! Did you imagine that Count Mancini would leave a woman when she needed help? *I* shall take her home—let your brutal heart be at rest—I shall take her home. Thomas, run for an automobile. Don't push me Briquet, you are as awkward as a unicorn . . . that's the way, that's the way——
[*They are holding her, guiding her slowly toward the door.* Consuelo, *her chin resting in her hand, is following them with her eyes. Unconsciously she assumes a somewhat affected pose.*]

Mancini

I'll come back for you, child——
[*Only* HE *and* Consuelo *are left on the stage. In the ring, music, shrieks, and laughter begin again.*]

He

Consuelo——

Consuelo

Is that you, He, dear?

He

Where did you learn that pose? I have seen it only in marble. You look like Psyche.

Consuelo

I don't know, HE. [*She sighs and sits on the sofa, keeping in her pose the same artificiality and beauty.*] It's all so sad here, to-day. HE, are you sorry for ZINIDA?

HE

What did she do?

Consuelo

I didn't see. I had closed my eyes, and didn't open them. Alfred says she is a wicked woman, but that isn't true. She has such nice eyes, and what tiny cold hands—as if she were dead. What does she do it for? Alfred says she should be audacious, beautiful, but quiet, otherwise what she does is only disgusting. It isn't true, is it, HE?

HE

She loves Alfred.

Consuelo

Alfred? My Bezano? [*Shrugging her shoulders, and surprised*] How does she love him? The same as everyone loves?

HE

Yes—as everyone loves—or still more.

CONSUELO

Bezano? Bezano? No—it's nonsense. [*Pause; silence.*] What a beautiful costume you have, HE. You invented it yourself?

HE

Jim helped me.

CONSUELO

Jim is so nice! All clowns are nice.

HE

I am wicked.

CONSUELO

[*Laughs*]: You? You are the nicest of all. Oh, goodness! Three acts more! This is the second on now. Alfred and I are in the third. Are you coming to see me?

HE

I always do. How beautiful you are, Consuelo.

CONSUELO

Like Eve? [*Smiles.*]

HE

Yes, Consuelo. And if the Baron asks you to be his wife, will you accept?

CONSUELO

Certainly, HE. That's all Father and I are waiting for. Father told me yesterday that the Baron will not hesitate very long. Of course I do not love him. But I will be his honest, faithful wife. Father wants to teach me to play the piano.

HE

Are those your own words—"his honest, faithful wife"?

CONSUELO

Certainly they are mine. Whose could they be? He loves me so much, the poor thing. Dear HE, what does "love" mean? Everybody speaks of love— love—Zinida, too! Poor Zinida! What a boring evening this has been! HE, did you paint the laughter on your face yourself?

HE

My own self, dear little Consuelo——

CONSUELO

How do you do it, all of you? I tried once, but couldn't do a thing. Why are there no women clowns? Why are you so silent, HE? You, too, are sad, to-night.

HE

No, I am happy to-night. Give me your hand, Consuelo, I want to see what it says.

CONSUELO

Do you know how? What a talented man you are! Read it, but don't *lie*, like a gypsy. [*He goes down on one knee and takes her hand. Both bend over it.*] Am I lucky?

HE

Yes, lucky. But wait a minute—this line here— funny. Ah, Consuelo, what does it say, here! [*Acting*] I tremble, my eyes do not dare to read the strange, fatal signs. Consuelo—

CONSUELO

The stars are talking.

HE

Yes, the stars are talking. Their voices are distant and terrible; their rays are pale, and their shadows slip by, like the ghosts of dead virgins—their spell is upon thee, Consuelo, beautiful Consuelo. Thou standest at the door of Eternity.

CONSUELO

I don't understand. Does it mean that I will live long?

HE

This line—how far it goes. Strange! Thou wilt live eternally, Consuelo.

CONSUELO

You see, HE, you did tell me a lie, just like a gypsy!

HE

But it is written—here, silly—and here. Now think of what the stars are saying. Here you have eternal life, love, and glory; and here, listen to what Jupiter says. He says: "Goddess, thou must not belong to any one born on earth," and if you marry the Baron—you'll perish, you'll die, Consuelo. [*Consuelo laughs.*]

Consuelo

Will he eat me?

He

No. But you will die before he has time to eat you.

Consuelo

And what will become of Father? Is there nothing about him here? [*Laughing, she softly sings the melody of the waltz, which is playing in the distance.*]

He

Don't laugh, Consuelo, at the voice of the stars. They are far away, their rays are light and pale, and we can barely see their sleeping shadows, but their sorcery is stern and dark. You stand at the gates of eternity. Your die is cast; you are *doomed*—and your Alfred, whom you love in your heart, even though your mind is not aware of it, your Alfred cannot save you. He, too, is a stranger on this earth. He is submerged in a deep sleep. He, too, is a little god who has lost himself, and Consuelo, never, never will he find his way to Heaven again. Forget Bezano——

Consuelo

I don't understand a word. Do the gods really exist? My teacher told me about them. But I thought it was all tales! [*Laughs.*] And my Bezano is a god?

HE

Forget Bezano! Consuelo, do you know who can save you? The only one who can save you? I.

CONSUELO

[*Laughing*]: You, HE?

HE

Yes, but don't laugh! Look. Here is the letter H. It is I, HE.

CONSUELO

HE Who Gets Slapped? Is that written here, too?

HE

That, too. The stars know everything. But look here, what more is written about him. Consuelo, welcome him. HE is an old god in disguise, who came down to earth only to love you, foolish little Consuelo.

CONSUELO

[*Laughing and singing*]: Some god!

HE

Don't mock! The gods don't like such empty laughter from beautiful lips. The gods grow lonely and die, when they are not recognized. Oh, Consuelo! Oh, great joy and love! Do recognize this god, and accept him. Think a moment, one day a god suddenly went crazy!

CONSUELO

Gods go crazy, too?

HE

Yes, when they are half man, then they often go mad. Suddenly he saw his own sublimity, and shuddered with horror, with infinite solitude, with superhuman anguish. It is terrible, when anguish touches the divine soul!

CONSUELO

I don't like it. What language are you speaking? I don't understand——

HE

I speak the language of thy awakening. Consuelo, recognize and accept thy god, who was thrown down from the summit like a stone. Accept the god who fell to the earth in order to live, to play, and to be infinitely drunk with joy. Evoë Goddess!

CONSUELO

[*Tortured*]: HE— I cannot understand. Let my hand alone.

HE

[*Stands up*]: Sleep. Then wake again, Consuelo! And when thou wakest—remember that hour when, covered with snow-white sea-foam, thou didst emerge from the sky-blue waters. Remember heaven, and the slow eastern wind, and the whisper of the foam at thy marble feet.

CONSUELO

[*Her eyes are closed*]: I believe—wait—I remember. Remind me further——
[*HE is bowed over* CONSUELO, *with lifted arms; he speaks slowly, but in a commanding voice, as if conjuring.*]

HE

You see the waves playing. Remember the song of the sirens, their sorrowless song of joy. Their white bodies, shining blue through the blue waters. Or can

you hear the sun, singing? Like the strings of a
divine harp, spread the golden rays— Do you not
see the hand of God, which gives harmony, light, and
love to the world? Do not the mountains, in the blue
cloud of incense, sing their hymn of glory? Remember, O Consuelo, remember the prayer of the mountains, the prayer of the sea. [*Silence.*]

HE

[*Commandingly*]: Remember—Consuelo!

CONSUELO

[*Opening her eyes*]: No! HE, I was feeling so
happy, and suddenly I forgot it all. Yet something
of it all is still in my heart. Help me again, HE,
remind me. It hurts, I hear so many voices. They
all sing "Consuelo—Consuelo." What comes after?
[*Silence; pause.*] What comes after? It hurts. Remind me, HE. [*Silence—in the ring, the music suddenly bursts forth in a tempestuous circus gallop.
Silence.*] HE, [*opens her eyes and smiles*] that's Alfred galloping. Do you recognize his music?

HE

[*With rage*]: Leave the boy alone! [*Suddenly
falls on his knees before* CONSUELO.] I love you, Consuelo, revelation of my heart, light of my nights, I

love you, Consuelo. [*Looks at her in ecstasy and tears—and gets a slap; starting back.*] What's this?

CONSUELO

A slap! You forget who you are. [*Stands up, with anger in her eyes.*] You are HE Who Gets Slapped! Did you forget it? Some god! With such a face—slapped face! Was it with slaps they threw you down from heaven, god?

HE

Wait! Don't stand up! I—did not finish the play!

CONSUELO

[*Sits*]: Then you were playing?

HE

Wait! One minute.

CONSUELO

You lied to me. Why did you play so that I believed you?

HE

I am HE Who Gets Slapped!

CONSUELO

You are not angry because I struck you? I did not want to really, but you were so—disgusting. And now you are so funny again. You have great talent, HE—or are you drunk?

HE

Strike me again.

CONSUELO

No.

HE

I need it for my play. Strike!

CONSUELO

[*Laughs, and touches his cheek with her finger-tips*]: Here, then!

HE

Didn't you understand that you are a queen, and I a fool who is in love with his queen? Don't you know, Consuelo, that every queen has a fool, and he is always in love with her, and they always beat him for it. HE Who Gets Slapped.

CONSUELO

No. I didn't know.

HE

Yes, every queen. Beauty has her fool. Wisdom, too. Oh, how many fools she has! Her court is over-crowded with enamoured fools, and the sound of slaps does not cease, even through the night. But I never received such a sweet slap as the one given by my little queen. [*Someone appears at the door. HE notices it, and continues to play, making many faces.*] Clown HE can have no rival! Who is there who could stand such a deluge of slaps, such a hail-storm of slaps, and not get soaked? [*Feigns to cry aloud.*] "Have pity on me. I am but a poor fool!"

[*Enter two men: an actor, dressed as a bareback rider, and a gentleman from the audience. He is spare, dressed in black, very respectable. He carries his hat in his hand.*]

CONSUELO

[*Laughing, embarrassed*]: HE, there is someone here. Stop!

HE

[*Gets up*]: Who is it? Who dares to intrude in the castle of my queen?

[*HE stops, suddenly. Consuelo, laughing, jumps up
and runs away, after a quick glance at the gentleman.*]

CONSUELO

You cheered me up, HE. Good-bye. [*At the door*]
You shall get a note to-morrow.

THE BAREBACK RIDER

[*Laughing*]: A jolly fellow, sir. You wanted to
see him? There he is. HE, the gentleman wants to see
you.

HE

[*In a depressed voice*]: What can I do for you?
[*The actor bows, and goes away, smiling. Both men
take a step toward each other.*]

GENTLEMAN

Is this you?

HE

Yes! It is I. And you? [*Silence.*]

GENTLEMAN

Must I believe my eyes? Is this *you*, Mr.——

He

[*In a rage*]: My name here is HE. I have no other name, do you hear? HE Who Gets Slapped. And if you want to stay here, don't forget it.

Gentleman

You are so familiar. As far as I can remember——

He

We are all familiar, here. [*Contemptuously*] Besides, that's all you deserve, anywhere.

Gentleman

[*Humbly*]: You have not forgiven me, HE? [*Silence.*]

He

Are you here with my wife? Is she, too, in the circus?

Gentleman

[*Quickly*]: Oh, no! I am alone. She stayed there!

He

You've left her already?

Gentleman

[*Humbly*]: No—we have—a son. After your sudden and mysterious disappearance—when you left that strange and insulting letter——

He

[*Laughs*]: Insulting? You are still able to feel insults? What are you doing here? Were you looking for me, or is it an accident?

Gentleman

I have been looking for you, for half a year—through many countries. And suddenly, to-day—by accident, indeed—I had no acquaintances here, and I went to the circus. We must talk things over . . . He, I implore you. [*Silence.*]

He

Here is a shadow I cannot lose! To talk things over! Do you really think we still have something to talk over? All right. Leave your address with the porter, and I will let you know when you can see me. Now get out. [*Proudly.*] I am busy.

[*The gentleman bows and leaves. HE does not return his bow, but stands with outstretched hand, in the pose of a great man, who shows a boring visitor the door.*]

Curtain

ACT III

*The same room.   Morning, before the rehearsal.
HE is striding thoughtfully up and down the room.
He wears a broad, parti-coloured coat, and a prismatic tie.   His derby is on the back of his head, and
his face is clean-shaven like that of an actor.   His
eyebrows are drawn, lips pressed together energeti-
cally, his whole appearance severe and sombre.   After
the entrance of the gentleman he changes.   His face
becomes clown-like, mobile—a living mask.*

*The gentleman comes in.   He is dressed in black,
and has an extremely well-bred appearance.   His thin
face is yellowish, like an invalid's.   When he is upset,
his colourless, dull eyes often twitch.   HE does not
notice him.*

GENTLEMAN

Good morning, sir.

HE

*[Turning around and looking at him absent-mind-
edly]*: Ah! It's you.

96

Gentleman

I am not late? You look as if you did not expect me. I hope I am not disturbing you? You fixed this time yourself however, and I took the liberty——

He

No manners, please. What do you want? Tell me quickly, I have no time.

Gentleman

[*Looking around with distaste*]: I expected you would invite me to some other place . . . to your home.

He

I have no other home. This is my home.

Gentleman

But people may disturb us here.

He

So much the worse for you. Talk faster! [*Silence.*]

Gentleman

Will you allow me to sit down?

He

Sit down. Look out! That chair is broken.

[*The gentleman, afraid, pushes away the chair and looks helplessly around. Everything here seems to him dangerous and strange. He chooses an apparently solid little gilded divan, and sits down; puts his silk hat aside, slowly takes off his gloves, which stick to his fingers. HE observes him indifferently.*]

Gentleman

In this suit, and with this face, you make a still stranger impression. Yesterday it seemed to me that it was all a dream; to-day . . . *you* . . .

He

You have forgotten my name again? My name is He.

Gentleman

You are determined to continue talking to me like this?

He

Decidedly! But you are squandering your time like a millionaire. Hurry up!

GENTLEMAN

I really don't know . . . Everything here strikes
me so . . . These posters, horses, animals, which
I passed when I was looking for you . . . And
finally, *you*, a clown in a circus! [*With a slight,
deprecating smile.*] Could I expect it? It is true,
when everybody there decided that you were dead, I
was the only man who did not agree with them. I
felt that you were still alive. But to find you among
such surroundings—I can't understand it.

HE

You said you have a son, now. Doesn't he look
like me?

GENTLEMAN

I don't understand?

HE

Don't you know that widows or divorced women
often have children by the new husband, which resemble the old one? This misfortune did not befall
you? [*Laughs.*] And your book, too, is a big success, I hear.

GENTLEMAN

You want to insult me again?

HE

[*Laughing*]: What a restless, touchy faker you are! Please sit still; be quiet. It is the custom here to speak this way. Why were you trying to find me?

GENTLEMAN

My conscience . . .

HE

You have no conscience. Or were you afraid that you hadn't robbed me of *everything* I possessed, and you came for the rest? But what more could you take from me now? My fool's cap with its bells? You wouldn't take it. It's too big for your bald head! Crawl back, you book-worm!

GENTLEMAN

You cannot forgive the fact that your wife . . .

HE

To the devil with my wife! [*The gentleman is startled and raises his eyebrows. HE laughs.*]

GENTLEMAN

I don't know. . . . But such language! I confess I find difficulty in expressing my thoughts in such an atmosphere, but if you are so . . . in-different to your wife, who, I shall allow myself to emphasize the fact, loved you and thought you were a saint—— [*HE laughs.*] Then *what* brought you to such a . . . step? Or is it that you cannot for-give me my success? A success, it is true, not entirely deserved. And now you want to take vengeance, with your humbleness, on those who misunderstood you. But you always were so indifferent to glory. Or your indifference was only hypocrisy. And when I, a more lucky rival . . .

HE

[*With a burst of laughter*]: Rival! You—a rival!

GENTLEMAN

[*Growing pale*]: But my book!

HE

You are talking to me about *your* book? To me? [*The gentleman is very pale. HE looks at him with curiosity and mockery.*]

GENTLEMAN

[*Raising his eyes*]: I am a very unhappy man.

HE

Why?

GENTLEMAN

I am a very unhappy man. You must forgive me. I am deeply, irreparably, and infinitely unhappy.

HE

But why? Explain it to me. [*Starts walking up and down.*] You say yourself that your book is a tremendous success, you are famous, you have glory; there is not a yellow newspaper in which *you* and *your* thoughts are not mentioned. Who knows *me?* Who cares about my heavy abstractions, from which it was difficult for them to derive a single thought? You— you are the great vulgarizer! You have made my thoughts comprehensible even to horses! With the art of a great vulgarizer, a tailor of ideas, you dressed my Apollo in a barber's jacket, you handed my Venus a yellow ticket, and to my bright hero you gave the ears of an ass. And then your career is made, as Jackson says. And wherever I go, the whole street looks at me with thousands of faces, in which—what mockery—I recognize the traits of my own children. Oh! How ugly your son must be, if he resembles me! Why then are you unhappy, you poor devil? [*The gentleman bows his head, plucking at his gloves.*]

The police haven't caught you, as yet. What am I talking about? Is it possible to catch you? You always keep within the limits of the law. You have been torturing yourself up to now because you are not married to my wife. A notary public is always present at your thefts. What is the use of this self-torture, my friend? Get married. I died. You are not satisfied with having taken only my wife? Let my glory remain in your possession. It is yours. Accept my ideas. Assume all the rights, my most lawful heir! I died! And when I was dying [*making a stupidly pious face*] I forgave thee! [*Bursts out laughing. The gentleman raises his head, and bending forward, looks straight into HE's eyes.*]

GENTLEMAN

And my pride?

HE

Have you any pride? [*The gentleman straightens up, and nods his head silently.*] Yes! But please stand off a little. I don't like to look at you. Think of it. There was a time when I loved you a little, even thought you a little gifted! You—my empty shadow.

GENTLEMAN

[*Nodding his head*]: I am your shadow. [*HE keeps on walking, and looks over his shoulder at the gentleman, with a smile.*]

He

Oh, you are marvellous! What a comedy! What a touching comedy! Listen. Tell me frankly if you can; do you hate me very much?

Gentleman

Yes! With all the hate there is in the world! Sit down here.

He

You order me?

Gentleman

Sit down here. Thank you. [*Bows.*] I am respected and I am famous, yes? I have a wife and a son, yes. [*Laughs slowly.*] My wife still loves you: our favourite discussion is about your genius. She supposes you are a genius. We, I and she, love you even when we are in bed. Tss! It is I who must make faces. My son—yes, he'll resemble you. And when, in order to have a little rest, I go to my desk, to my ink-pot, my books—there, too, I find you. Always you! Everywhere you! And I am never alone —never myself and alone. And when at night—you, sir, should understand this—when at night I go to my lonely thoughts, to my sleepless contemplations, even then I find your image in my head, in my unfortunate brain, your damned and hateful image! [*Silence. The gentleman's eyes twitch.*]

HE

[*Speaking slowly*]: What a comedy. How marvellously everything is turned about in this world: the robbed proves to be a robber, and the robber is complaining of theft, and cursing! [*Laughs.*] Listen, I was mistaken. You are not my shadow. You are the crowd. If you live by my creations, you hate me; if you breathe my breath, you are choking with anger. And choking with anger, hating me, you still walk slowly on the trail of my ideas. But you are advancing backward, advancing backward, comrade! Oh, what a marvellous comedy! [*Walking and smiling.*] Tell me, would you be relieved if I really had died?

GENTLEMAN

Yes! I think so. Death augments distance and dulls the memory. Death reconciles. But you do not look like a man who——

HE·

Yes, yes! Death, *certainly!*

Gentleman

Sit down here.

He

Your obedient servant. Yes?

Gentleman

Certainly, I do not dare to ask you—[*makes a grimace*] to ask you to die, but tell me: you'll never come back there? No, don't laugh. If you want me to, I'll kiss your hand. Don't grimace! I would have done so if you had died.

He

[*Slowly*]: Get out, vermin!
[*Enter Tilly and Polly as in the first act, playing. For a long time they do not see the two men.*]

He

Jack!

Tilly

Ah! Good morning, HE. We are rehearsing. You know it is very hard. Jack has just about as much music in his head as my pig.

HE

[*Introducing, nonchalantly*]: My friend . . . For the benefit performance? [*The clowns bow to the gentleman, making idiotic faces.*]

POLLY

Yes. What are you preparing? You are cunning, HE! Consuelo told me what you are preparing for the benefit performance. She leaves us soon, you know?

HE

Is that so?

TILLY

Zinida told us. Do you think she would get a benefit performance otherwise? She is a nice girl.

POLLY

[*Taking his small flute-pipe*]: Here! Don't walk as if you were an elephant. Don't forget you are an ant! Come on! [*They go off, playing.*]

GENTLEMAN

[*Smiling*]: These are your new comrades? How strange they are!

HE

Everything here is strange.

GENTLEMAN

This suit of yours. Black used to be very becoming to you. This one hurts the eyes.

HE

[*Looking himself over*]: Why? It looks very nice. The rehearsal has begun. You must go away. You are disturbing us.

GENTLEMAN

You did not answer my question.
[*Slow strains of the Tango from a small orchestra in the ring.*]

HE

[*Listening absent-mindedly to the music*]: What question?

GENTLEMAN

[*Who does not hear the music*]: I pray you to tell me: will you ever come back?

HE

[*Listening to the music*]: Never, never, never!

Gentleman

[*Getting up*]: Thank you. I am going.

He

Never, never, never! Yes, run along. And don't come back. There you were still bearable and useful for something, but here you are superfluous.

Gentleman

But if something should happen to you . . . you are a healthy man, but in this environment, these people . . . how will I know? They don't know your name here?

He

My name here is unknown, but *you will know*. Anything else?

Gentleman

I can be at peace? On your word of honour? Of course I mean, comparatively, at peace?

He

Yes, you may be comparatively at peace. Never! [*They walk to the door, the gentleman stops.*]

Gentleman

May I come to the circus? You will allow me?

He

Certainly. You are the audience! [*Laughs.*] But I shan't give you my card for a pass. But why do you want to come? Or do you like the circus so much, and since when?

Gentleman

I want to look at you some more, and to understand, perhaps. Such a transformation! Knowing you as I do, I cannot admit that you are here without any *idea*. But what idea? [*Looks short-sightedly at HE. HE grimaces and thumbs his nose.*]

Gentleman

What is that?

He

My idea! Good-bye, Prince! My regards to your respected wife, your Highness' wonderful son!
[*Enter* Mancini.]

Mancini

You positively live in the circus, He. Whenever I come, you are here. You are a fanatic in your work, sir.

HE

[*Introducing*]: Prince Poniatovsky, Count Mancini.

MANCINI

[*Drawing himself up*]: Very, very glad. And you too, Prince, you know my queer fellow? What a nice face he has, hasn't he? [*He touches HE'S shoulder patronizingly, with the tip of his cane.*]

GENTLEMAN

[*Awkwardly*]: Yes, I have the pleasure . . . certainly. Good-bye, Count.

MANCINI

Good-day, Prince.

HE

[*Accompanying him*]: Look out, your Highness, for the dark passages: the steps are so rotten. Unfortunately I cannot usher you out to the street.

GENTLEMAN

[*In a low voice*]: You will not give me your hand when we say good-bye? We are parting for ever.

HE

Unnecessary, Prince. I shall still hope to meet you in the Kingdom of Heaven. I trust you will be there, too?

GENTLEMAN

[*With disgust*]: How you did succeed! You have so much of the clown in you!

HE

I am HE Who is Getting Slapped. Good-bye, Prince. [*They take another step.*]

GENTLEMAN

[*Looking HE in the eyes; in a very low voice*]: Tell me, you are not mad?

HE

[*Just as low, his eyes wide open*]: I am afraid, I am afraid you are right, Prince. [*Still low*] Ass! Never in your life did you use such a precise expression. I am mad!

[*Playing the clown again, he shows him to the stair, with a big, affected gesture, a sweep of the hand and arm from his head to the floor, the fingers moving, to represent the steps.*]

HE

[*Laughing*]: He is down! *Au revoir*, Prince. [*The gentleman goes out. HE comes skipping back, and takes a pose.*] Mancini! Let us dance the Tango! Mancini, I adore you!

MANCINI

[*Sitting back comfortably and playing with his cane*]: Don't forget yourself, HE. But you're hiding something, my boy. I always said you used to belong to society. It is so easy to talk to you. And who is this Prince? A genuine one?

HE

Genuine. A first-rater. Like you!

MANCINI

A sympathetic face. Although at first I thought he was an undertaker who came for an order. Ah, HE! When shall I finally depart from these dirty walls, from Papa Briquet, stupid posters, and brutal jockeys!

HE

Very soon, Mancini.

Mancini

Yes, soon. I am simply exhausted in these surroundings, He! I begin to feel myself a horse. You are from society, still you don't yet know what high society means. To be at last decently dressed, to attend receptions, to display the splendour of wit; from time to time to have a game of baccarat [*laughing*] without tricks or cheating——

He

And when evening comes, go to a suburb, where you are considered an honest father, who loves his children and——

Mancini

And get hold of something, eh? [*Laughs.*] I shall wear a silk mask and two butlers shall follow me, thus protecting me from the dirty crowd. Ah, He! The blood of my ancestors boils in me. Look at this stiletto. What do you think? Do you think that it was ever stained with blood?

He

You frighten me, Count!

Mancini

[*Laughing, and putting the stiletto back into its sheath*]: Fool!

HE

And what about the girl?

MANCINI

Tss! I give those bourgeois absolute satisfaction, and they glorify my name. [*Laughs.*] The splendour of my name is beginning to shine with a force unknown. By the way, do you know what automobile firms are the best? Money is no object. [*Laughs.*] Ah! Papa Briquet!

[*Enter Briquet in his overcoat and silk hat. They shake hands.*]

BRIQUET

So, Mancini, you have obtained a benefit performance for your daughter, Consuelo! I only want to tell you, that if it were not for Zinida . . .

MANCINI

Listen, Briquet. Decidedly you are a donkey. What are you complaining of? The Baron has bought all the parquet seats for Consuelo's benefit performance. Isn't that enough for you, you miser?

BRIQUET

I love your daughter, Mancini, and I am sorry to let her go. What more does she need here? She has an honest job, wonderful comrades, and the atmosphere—?

MANCINI

Not *she*, but *I* need something. You understand?
[*Laughs.*] I asked you to increase her salary, Harpagon! and now, Mr. Manager, wouldn't you like to change me a thousand franc note?

BRIQUET

[*With a sigh*]: Give it to me.

MANCINI

[*Nonchalantly*]: To-morrow. I left it at home.
[*All three laugh.*] Laugh, laugh! To-day we are going with the Baron to his villa in the country; people say a very nice villa.

HE

What for?

MANCINI

You know, HE, the crazes of these billionaires. He wants to show Consuelo some winter roses, and me his wine cellars. He will come for us here. What is the matter, my little Consuelo?
[*Enter* CONSUELO, *almost crying.*]

Consuelo

I can't father! Tell him! What right has he to yell at me? He almost hit me with his whip!

Mancini

[*Straightening up*]: Briquet! I beg of you, as the Manager, what is this—a stable? To hit my daughter with a whip! I'll show this cub . . . a mere jockey. . . . No, the devil knows what it is, devil knows, I swear. . . .

Consuelo

Father . . .

Briquet

I will tell him.

Consuelo

Please don't. Alfred didn't hit me. It's a silly thing, what I told you. What an idea! He is so sorry himself. . . .

Briquet

I shall tell him anyhow that——

Consuelo

Don't you dare. You mustn't tell him anything. He didn't do a thing.

Mancini

[*Still excited*] : He must beg her pardon, the brat.

Consuelo

He's already asked me to forgive him. How silly you all are! I simply cannot work to-day and I got nervous. What nonsense! The silly boy asked me to forgive him, but I didn't want to. He, dear, good morning! I didn't notice you. How becoming your tie is! Where are you going, Briquet? To Alfred?

Briquet

No, I am going home, dear child. Zinida asked me to give you her love. She will not be here to-day, either. [*He goes out.*]

Consuelo

Zinida is so nice, so good. Father, why is it that everybody seems so nice to me? Probably because I am going away soon. He, did you hear the march that Tilly and Polly will play? [*Laughs.*] Such a cheerful one.

He

Yes. I heard it. Your benefit performance will be remarkable.

CONSUELO

I think so, too. Father I am hungry. Have them bring me a sandwich.

HE

I'll run for it, my Queen.

CONSUELO

Please do, HE. [*Loudly*] But not cheese. I don't like it.

[MANCINI *and* CONSUELO *are alone.* MANCINI, *lying back comfortably in an armchair, scrutinizes his daughter with a searching eye.*]

MANCINI

I find something particular in you to-day, my child. I don't know whether it is something better or worse. You cried?

CONSUELO

Yes, a little. Oh, I am so hungry.

MANCINI

But you had your breakfast?

Consuelo

No, I didn't. That's why I am so hungry. You
again forgot to leave me some money this morning,
and without money . . .

Mancini

Oh, the devil . . . what a memory I have.
[*Laughs.*] But we shall have a very nice meal to-day.
Don't eat very many sandwiches. . . . Yes, positively I like you. You must cry more often, my child;
it washes off your superfluous simplicity. You become more of a woman.

Consuelo

Am I so simple, Father?

Mancini

Very. . . . Too much. I like it in others, but
not in you. Besides, the Baron . . .

Consuelo

Nonsense. I am not simple. But you know, Bezano scolded me so much, that even you would have
cried. The devil knows . . .

MANCINI

Tsss. . . . Never say "the devil knows." It isn't decent.

CONSUELO

I say it only when I am with you.

MANCINI

You must not say it when you are with me, either. I know it without you. [*Laughs.*]

CONSUELO

Ha! Listen, Father! It's a new number of Alfred's. He makes such a jump! Jim says he's bound to break his neck. Poor fish. . . .

MANCINI

[*Indifferently*]: Or his leg, or his back; they all have to break something. [*Laughs.*] They are breakable toys.

CONSUELO

[*Listening to the music*]: I'll be lonesome without them, Father! The Baron promised to make a ring for me to gallop over as much as I want. He's not lying?

MANCINI

A ring? [*Laughs.*] No, it's not a lie. By the way, child, when speaking of Barons, you must say, "he does not tell the truth," and not, "he lies."

CONSUELO

It's just the same. It's nice to be wealthy, Father; you can do what you want, then.

MANCINI

[*With enthusiasm*]: Everything you want. Everything, my child. Ah! Our fate is being decided to-day. Pray our clement God, Consuelo. The Baron is hanging on a thread.

CONSUELO

[*Indifferently*]: Yes?

MANCINI

[*Making the gesture with his fingers*]: On a very thin, silk thread. I am almost sure that he will make his proposal to-day. [*Laughs.*] Winter roses, and the web of a spider amongst the roses, in order that my dear little fly . . . He is such a spider.

Consuelo

[*Indifferently*]: Yes, a terrible spider. Father, oughtn't I to let him kiss my hand yet?

By no means. You don't know yet, darling, what these men are.

Consuelo

Alfred never kisses.

Mancini

Alfred! Your Alfred is a cub, and he mustn't dare. But with men of that sort, you must be extremely careful, my child. To-day he would kiss your little finger, to-morrow your hand, and after to-morrow you would be on his lap.

Consuelo

Foui! Father, what are you talking about? You should be ashamed!

Mancini

But I know. . . .

Consuelo

Don't you dare! I don't want to hear such dirty things. I shall give the Baron such a slap! A better one than HE—let him only try.

Mancini

[*With a deprecating gesture*]: All men are like that, child.

Consuelo

It isn't true. Alfred is not. Ah! But where is HE? He said he'd run, and he hasn't come back.

Mancini

The buffet here is closed, and he has to get the sandwiches somewhere else. Consuelo, as your father, I want to warn you about HE. Don't trust him. He knows something. [*Twirls his finger close to his forehead.*] His game is not fair.

Consuelo

You say it about everybody. I know HE; he is such a nice man, and he loves me so much.

Mancini

Believe me, there is something in it.

Consuelo

Father, you make me sick with your advice.   Ah!
He, thank you.

[*HE, breathing somewhat heavily, enters and gives
her the sandwiches.*]

He

Eat, Consuelo.

Consuelo

A hot one.   .   .   .   But you were running, He?
I am so grateful.   [*Eats.*]   He, do you love me?

He

I do, my Queen.   I am your court fool.

Consuelo

[*Eating*]: And when I leave, will you find another
queen?

He

[*Making a ceremonious bow*]: I shall follow after
you, my incomparable one.   I shall carry the train of
your dress and wipe away my tears with it.   [*Pre-
tends to cry.*]

MANCINI

Idiot! [*Laughs.*] How sorry I am, HE, that
those wonderful times have passed, when, in the court
of the Counts Mancini, there were scores of motley
fools who were given gold and kicks. . . . Now,
Mancini is compelled to go to this dirty circus in
order to see a good fool; and still, whose fool is he?
Mine? No. He belongs to everybody who pays a
franc. We shall very soon be unable to breathe because of Democracy. Democracy, too, needs fools!
Think of it, HE; what an unexampled impertinence.

HE

We are the servants of those who pay. But how
can we help it, Count?

MANCINI

But is that not sad? Imagine: we are in my castle.
I, near the fireplace with my glass of wine, you, at
my feet chatting your nonsense, jingling your little
bells—diverting me. Sometimes you pinch me too
with your jokes: it is allowed by the traditions and
necessary for the circulation of the blood. After a
while—I am sick of you, I want another one. . . .
Then I give you a kick and . . . Ah, HE, how
wonderful it would be!

He

It would be marvellous, Mancini!

Mancini

Yes. Certainly! You would be getting gold coins, those wonderfully little yellow things. . . . Well, when I become rich, I shall take you. That's settled.

Consuelo

Take him, Father . . .

He

And when the count, tired of my chattering, will give me a kick with his Highness's foot, then I shall lie down at the little feet of my queen, and shall . . .

Consuelo

[*Laughing*]: Wait for another kick? I'm finished. Father, give me your handkerchief, I want to wipe my hands. You have another one in your pocket. Oh, my goodness, I must work some more!

Mancini

[*Uneasy*]: But don't forget, my child!

CONSUELO

No, to-day I won't forget! Go on!

MANCINI

[*Looking at his watch*]: Yes, it is time. . . .
He asked me to come over when you were ready. You
must change your dress before I come back. [*Laughing.*] *Signori, miei complimenti.*
[*He goes out, playing with his cane.* CONSUELO *sits
on the corner of the divan, and covers herself
with her shawl.*]

CONSUELO

Hello, HE! Come and lie down at my feet, and tell
me something cheerful. . . . You know, when you
paint the laughter on your face, you are very good
looking, but now, too, you are very, very nice. Come
on, HE, why don't you lie down?

HE

Consuelo! Are you going to marry the Baron?

CONSUELO

[*Indifferently*]: It seems so. The Baron is hanging by a thread! HE, there is one little sandwich left.
Eat it.

HE

Thank you, my queen. [*Eats.*] And do you remember my prediction?

CONSUELO

What prediction? How quickly you swallow! Does it taste good?

HE

Very good. That if you marry the Baron, you . . .

CONSUELO

Oh, that's what you're talking about. . . . But you were making fun.

HE

Nobody can tell, my Queen. Sometimes one makes fun, and suddenly it turns out to be true; the stars never talk in vain. If sometimes it is difficult for a human being to open his mouth and to say a word, how difficult it must be for a star. Think of it.

CONSUELO

[*Laughing*]: I should say. Such a mouth! [*Makes a tiny mouth.*]

He

No, my dear little girl, were I in your place, I would think it over. And suppose suddenly you should die? Don't marry the Baron, Consuelo!

Consuelo

[*Thinking*]: And what is—death?

He

I do not know, my Queen. Nobody knows. Like love! Nobody knows. But your little hands will become cold, and your dear little eyes will be closed. You will be away from here. And the music will play without you, and without you the crazy Bezano will be galloping, and Tilly and Polly will be playing on their pipes without you: tilly-polly, tilly-polly . . . tilly-tilly, polly-polly . . .

Consuelo

Please don't, He darling—— I am so sad, anyway . . . tilly-tilly, polly-polly . . . [*Silence. HE looks at* Consuelo.]

He

You were crying, my little Consuelo?

Consuelo

Yes, a little. Alfred made me nervous. But tell me, is it my fault that I can't do anything to-day? I tried to, but I couldn't.

He

Why?

Consuelo

Ah, I don't know. There is something here. [*Presses her hand against her heart.*] I don't know. He, I must be sick. What is sickness? Does it hurt very much?

He

It is not sickness. It is the charm of the far off stars, Consuelo. It is the voice of your fate, my little Queen.

Consuelo

Don't talk nonsense, please. What should the stars care about me? I am so small. Nonsense, He! Tell me rather another tale which you know: about the blue sea and those gods, you know . . . who are so beautiful. Did they all die?

HE

They are all alive, but they hide themselves, my goddess.

CONSUELO

In the woods or mountains? Can one come across them? Ah, imagine HE . . . I come across a god, and he suddenly takes a look at me! I'd run away. [*Laughs.*] This morning when I went without breakfast, I became so sad, so disgusted, and I thought: if a god should come, and give me something to eat! And as I thought it, I suddenly heard, honestly it's true, I heard: "Consuelo, somebody's calling you." [*Angrily.*] Don't you dare laugh!

HE

Am I laughing?

CONSUELO

Honestly, it's true. Ah, HE, but he didn't come. He only called me and disappeared, and how can you find him? It hurt me so much, and hurts even now. Why did you remind me of my childhood? I'd forgotten it entirely. There was the sea . . . and something . . . many, many [*closes her eyes, smiling.*]

HE

Remember, Consuelo.

CONSUELO

No. [*Opening her eyes*] I forget everything about it. [*Looks around the room.*] He, do you see what a poster they made for my benefit performance? It's Father's idea. The Baron liked it. [*HE laughs. Silence.*]

HE

[*Slowly*] Consuelo, my Queen! Don't go to the Baron to-day.

CONSUELO

Why? [*After a silence.*] How fresh you are, HE.

HE

[*Lowering his head, slowly*]: I don't want it.

CONSUELO

[*Getting up*]: What? You don't want it?

HE

[*Bowing his head still lower*]: I do not want you to marry the Baron [*Imploring.*] I . . . I shall not allow it . . . I beg you!

CONSUELO

Whom, then, would you ask me to marry? You, perhaps, you fool? [*With a rancorous laugh*] Are

you crazy, my darling? "I shall not allow." HE!
HE will not allow me! But it is unbearable! What
business is it of yours? [*Walking up and down the
room, looks over her shoulder at HE, with anger.*]
Some fool clown, whom they can kick out of here
any minute. You make me sick with your stupid
tales. Or you like slaps so much. Fool, you couldn't
invent anything better than a slap!

HE

[*Without lifting his head*]: Forgive me, my
Queen.

CONSUELO

He is glad when they laugh at him. Some god!
No, I shan't forgive. I know you. [*Makes same
gesture as* MANCINI.] You have something there!
Laughs . . . so nicely . . . plays, plays, and then
suddenly—hop! *Obey him!* No, darling, I am not
that kind! Carry my train, that is your business—
fool!

HE

I shall carry your train, my Queen. Forgive me.
Give me back the image of my beautiful, piteous
goddess.

Consuelo

[*Quieting down*]: You're playing again?

He

I am.

Consuelo

[*Laughing*]: You see! [*Sits down.*] Foolish He.

He

I see everything, my Queen. I see how beautiful you are, and how low under your feet your poor court fool is lying. Somewhere in the abyss his little bells are ringing. He kneels before you and prays; forgive and pity him, my divine one. He was too impudent; he played so cheerfully that he went too far and lost his tiny little mind, the last bit of understanding he had saved up. Forgive me!

Consuelo

All right. I forgive you. [*Laughs.*] And now will you allow me to marry the Baron?

He

[*Also laughing*]: And nevertheless I will not allow it. But what does a queen care about the permission of her enamoured fool?

CONSUELO

Get up. You are forgiven. And do you know why? You think because of your words? You are a cunning beast, HE! No, because of the *sandwiches*. That's why. You were so lovely, you panted so when you brought them. Poor darling HE. From to-morrow you may be at my feet again. And as soon as I whistle, "tuwhooo"——

HE

I shall instantly lie down at thy feet, Consuelo. It is settled! But all my little bells fell off to-day and——

[*Bezano appears, confused.*]

CONSUELO

Alfred! You came for me?

BEZANO

Yes. Will you work some more, Consuelo?

CONSUELO

Certainly. As much as you want. But I thought, Alfred, you were mad at me? I shan't dawdle any more.

Bezano

No. You didn't dawdle. Don't be offended, because I yelled so much. You know when one has to teach, and——

Consuelo

My goodness, do you think I don't understand? You are too nice, unbearably nice, to like teaching such a fool as me. Do you think I don't understand? Come on!

Bezano

Come on! Hello, He! I haven't seen you yet to-day. How are you?

He

How are you, Bezano? Wait, wait a minute— stay here a minute, both of you—that way. Yes!
[Consuelo *and* Bezano *stand side by side, the jockey scowling,* Consuelo *laughing and flushing.*]

Consuelo

Like Adam and Eve? How foolish you are! Terribly. [*She runs away.*] I shall only change my slippers, Alfred.

HE

Consuelo! And how about Father and the Baron? They will come soon, to take you with them.

CONSUELO

Let them come. They can wait. Not very important people. [*Runs away.* BEZANO *hesitatingly follows her.*]

HE

Stay here for a while, Bezano. Sit down.

BEZANO

What more do you want? I have no time for your nonsense.

HE

You can remain standing if you want. Bezano—you love her? [*Silence.*]

BEZANO

I shall allow nobody to interfere with my affairs. You allow yourself too many liberties, HE. I don't know you. You came from the street, and why should I trust you?

HE

But you know the Baron? Listen. It is painful for me to pronounce these words: she loves you. Save her from the spider! Or are you blind, and don't see the web, which is woven in every dark corner. Get out of the vicious circle in which you are turning around, like a blind man. Take her away, steal her, do what you want . . . kill her even, and take her to the heavens or to the devil! But don't give her to this man! He is a defiler of love. And if you are timid, if you are afraid to lift your hand against her—kill the Baron! Kill!

BEZANO

[*With a smile*]: And who will kill the others, to come?

HE

She loves you.

BEZANO

Did she tell you that herself?

HE

What a petty, what a stupid, what a human pride! But *you* are a little god! A god, youth! Why

don't you want to believe me? Or does the street,
from which I have come, bother you? But look,
look yourself. Look in my eyes, do such eyes lie?
Yes, my face is ugly, I make faces and grimaces, I
am surrounded by laughter, but don't you see the
god behind all this, a god, like you? Look, look at
me! [BEZANO *bursts out laughing*.] What are you
laughing at, youth?

BEZANO

You look now as you did that evening in the
ring. You remember? When you were a great
man, and they sent for you from the Academy, and
suddenly—Hup! HE Who Gets Slapped!

HE

[*Laughing the same way*]: Yes, yes, you are right,
Bezano. There is a resemblance. [*With a strained
expression, taking a pose*] "It seems to me they sent
for me from the Academy!"

BEZANO

[*Displeased*]: But I don't like this play. You
can present *your* face for slaps if you want to, but
don't dare to expose mine. [*Turns to go.*]

HE

Bezano!

Bezano

[*Turning round*]: And never let me hear any more about Consuelo, and don't dare to tell me again that I am a god! It is disgusting.

[Bezano *goes out angrily, striking his boot with his whip. HE is alone. Wrathfully, with a tortured expression, he makes a step towards the jockey, then stops, with soundless laughter, his head thrown backwards. The* Baron *and* Mancini *find him in this position, when they enter.*]

Mancini

[*Laughing*]: What a cheerful chap you are, He! You laugh when you are alone. [*HE laughs aloud.*] Stop it fool! How can you stand it?

He

[*Bowing low, with a large gesture*]: How do you do, Baron? My humblest respects to you, Count. I beg your pardon, Count, but you found the clown at work. These are, so to speak, Baron, his every-day pleasures.

Mancini

[*Lifting his eyebrows*]: Tsss. But you are a clever man, He. I shall ask Papa Briquet to give you a benefit performance. Shall I, He?

He

Please do me the favour, Count.

Mancini

Don't overdo. Be more simple, He. [*Laughs.*]
But how many slaps will you get at your benefit performance, when even on weekdays they ring you like
a gong! A funny profession, isn't it, Baron?

Baron

Very strange. But where is the Countess?

Mancini

Yes, yes. I shall go for her at once. Dear child,
she is so absorbed in her benefit performance and her
work. They call this jumping *work*, Baron.

Baron

I can wait a little. [*Sits down, with his silk hat
on his head.*]

Mancini

But why? I shall hurry her up. I shall be back
at once. And you, He, be a nice host, and entertain
our dear guest. You will not be bored in his company, Baron.

[*He goes out. HE strides about the stage, smiling
  and glancing from time to time at the* BARON.
  *The latter sits with his legs spread apart and
  his chin on the top of his cane. The silk hat
  remains on his head. He is silent.*]

HE

In what way would you like me to entertain you,
Baron?

BARON

In no way! I don't like clowns.

HE

Nor I Barons.
[*Silence. HE puts on his derby hat, takes a chair
  with a large gesture, and puts it down heavily,
  in front of the* BARON. *HE sits astride it,
  imitating the pose of the* BARON, *and looks him
  in the eyes. Silence.*]

HE

Can you be silent very long?

BARON

Very long.

HE

[*Taps on the floor with his foot*]: And can you wait very long?

BARON

Very long.

HE

Until you get it?

BARON

Until I get it.   And you?

HE

I too.

[*Both look at each other, silently, their heads close
together.   From the ring one hears the strains
of the Tango.*]

CURTAIN

ACT IV

Music in the ring. More disorder in the room than usual. All kinds of actors' costumes hanging on pegs and lying in the corners. On the table a bouquet of fiery-red roses, put there by some careless hand. At the entrance, near the arch, three bareback riders are smoking and chattering; they are all minor actors. All part their hair the same way; two wear small moustaches; the third one is clean-shaven with a face like a bull-dog.

The Clean-Shaven One

Go on, Henry! Ten thousand francs! It's too much even for the Baron.

The Second

How much are roses now?

The Shaven

I don't know. In winter they are certainly more expensive, but still Henry talks nonsense. Ten thousand!

The Second

The Baron has his own hothouse. They don't cost him anything.

Henry

[*Throwing away his cigar, which has burned the tips of his fingers*]: No, Grab, you're silly. There's a whole car-load full! One can smell the roses a mile away. They're to cover the entire arena.

The Shaven

Only the ring.

Henry

It's all the same. In order to cover the ring, you must have thousands and thousands of roses. You'll see what it looks like, when they've covered everything like a carpet. He ordered them to make it like a carpet! Do you see, Grab?

The Second

What a Baron's craze! Isn't it time yet?

Henry

No, we have time enough. I rather like it: a fiery-red tango on a fiery-red cover of winter roses!

The Shaven

Consuelo will be galloping on roses.   And Bezano?

The Second

And Bezano on thorns.   [*Smiles.*]

The Shaven

That youngster has no self-respect.   I'd have re-
fused.

Henry

But it is his job.   He's got to do it.   [*Laughs.*]
Talk to him about self-respect.   He's as angry and
proud as a little Satan.

The Second

No, you may say what you like, it's an excellent
benefit performance.   It's a joy to look at the crowd.
They're so excited.

Henry

Tss! [*All throw away their cigars and cigarettes,
like school boys who are caught, and make way for*
Zinida, *who enters with* HE.]

ZINIDA

What are you doing here, gentlemen? Your place is at the entrance.

HENRY

[*With a respectful smile*]: We are here just for a minute, Madame Zinida. We are going. What a successful evening! And what a glory for Papa Briquet!

ZINIDA

Yes. Go, and please don't leave your places. [*They go.* ZINIDA *pulls a drawer out of the desk, and puts in some papers. She is in her lion tamer's costume.*] HE, what were you doing near my lions? You frightened me.

HE

Why, Duchess, I merely wanted to hear what the beasts were saying about the benefit performance. They are pacing in their cages, and growling.

ZINIDA

The music makes them nervous. Sit down, HE. An excellent evening, and I am so glad that Consuelo is leaving us. Have you heard about the Baron's roses.

HE

Everybody is talking about them. The Hymeneal roses!

ZINIDA

Here are some, too. [*Pushes away the bouquet.*] You find them everywhere. Yes, I am glad. She is superfluous here, and disturbs our work. It is a misfortune for a cast to have in it such a beautiful and such an . . . accessible girl.

HE

But it is an honest marriage, Duchess, is it not?

ZINIDA

I don't care what it is.

HE

Spiders, too need an improvement in their breed! Can't you imagine, Zinida, what charming little spiders this couple will create! They will have the face of their mother, Consuelo, and the stomach of their father, the Baron, and thus could be an ornament for any circus-ring.

ZINIDA

You are malicious to-day, HE. You are morose.

He

I laugh.

Zinida

You do, but without joy. Why are you without make-up?

He

I am in the third act. I have time. And how does Bezano feel about this evening. Is he glad?

Zinida

I didn't talk to Bezano. You know what I think, my friend? You, too, are superfluous here. [*Silence.*]

He

How do you want me to take that, Zinida?

Zinida

Just as I said. In fact, Consuelo sold herself for nothing. What is the Baron worth, with his poor millions? People say that you are clever, too clever perhaps; tell me then, for how much could one buy me?

HE

[*Looking as if he were pricing her*]: Only for a crown.

ZINIDA

A baron's crown?

HE

No, a royal one.

ZINIDA

You are far from being stupid. And you guessed that Consuelo is not Mancini's daughter?

HE

[*Startled*]: What! And she knows it?

ZINIDA

Hardly. Why should she know it? Yes, she is a girl from Corsica whose parents are unknown. He preferred to use her for business rather than . . . But according to the law, she is his daughter, Countess Veronica Mancini.

HE

It is nice, to have everything done according to law, isn't it, Zinida? But it is curious there is more blue blood in her than in this Mancini. One would say that it was she who found him on the street, and made him a count and her father. Count Mancini! [*Laughs.*]

ZINIDA

Yes, you are gloomy, HE. I changed my mind, you'd better stay.

HE

Will I not be superfluous?

ZINIDA

When she is gone, you will not. Oh! You don't know yet, how nice it is to be with us. What a rest for the body and mind. I understand you. I am clever, too. Like you, I brought with me from out there my inclination for chains, and for a long time I chained myself to whatever I could, in order to feel firm.

HE

Bezano?

ZINIDA

Bezano and others; there were many, there will be many more. My red lion, with whom I am desperately

in love, is still more terrible than Bezano. But it is
all nonsense; old habits, which we are sorry to let
go. like old servants who steal things. Leave Consuelo alone. She has her own way.

HE

Automobiles and diamonds?

ZINIDA

When did you see a beauty clad in simple cotton?
If this one does not buy her, another will. They buy
off everything that is beautiful. Yes, I know. For
the first ten years she will be a sad beauty, who will
attract the eyes of the poor man on the side-walk:
afterward she will begin to paint a little around her
eyes and smile, and then will take——

HE

Her *chauffeur* or butler as a lover? You're not
guessing badly, Zinida!

ZINIDA

Am I not right? I don't want to intrude on
your confidence, but to-day I am sorry for you, HE.
What can you do against Fate? Don't be offended,
my friend, by the words of a woman. I like you; you

are not beautiful, nor young, nor rich, and your place is——

He

On the side-walk, from which one looks at the beauties. [*Laughs.*] And if I don't want to?

Zinida

What does it matter, your "want" or "don't want"? I am sorry for you, my poor friend, but if you are a strong man, and I think you are, then there is only one way for you. To forget.

He

You think that that's being strong? And you are saying this, you, Queen Zinida, who want to awaken the feeling of love, even in the heart of a lion? For one second of an illusory possession, you are ready to pay with your life, and still you advise me to forget! Give me your strong hand, my beautiful lady; see how much strength there is in this pressure, and don't pity me.

[*Enter* Briquet *and* Mancini. *The latter is reserved, and self-consciously imposing. He has a new suit, but the same cane, and the same noiseless smile of a satyr.*]

Zinida

[*Whispering*]: Will you stay?

He

Yes. I shan't go away.

Mancini

How are you, my dear? But you are dazzling, my dear! I swear you are marvellous! Your lion would be an ass, if he did not kiss your hand, as I do. . . . [*Kisses her hand.*]

Zinida

May I congratulate you, Count?

Mancini

Yes, *merci*. [*To HE*] How are you, my dear?

He

Good evening, Count!

Briquet

Zinida, the Count wants to pay immediately for the breach of contract with Consuelo . . . the Countess's contract. Don't you remember, Mother, how much it is?

Zinida

I'll look it up, Papa.

Mancini

Yes, please.   Consuelo will not return here any more.   We leave to-morrow.

[Zinida *and* Briquet *search among the papers.* HE *takes* Mancini *roughly by the elbow, and draws him aside.*]

He

[*In a low voice*]:   How are your girls, Mancini?

Mancini

What girls?   What is this, stupidity or blackmail? Look out, sir, be careful, the policeman is not far.

He

You are much too severe, Mancini.   I assumed, that since we are *tête-á-tête* . . .

Mancini

But tell me, what kind of *tête-á-tête* is possible, between a clown and me?   [*Laughs.*]   You are stupid, He.   You should say what you want, and not ask questions!

BRIQUET

Three thousand francs, Count.

MANCINI

Is that all? For Consuelo? All right. I'll tell
the Baron.

ZINIDA

You took——

BRIQUET

Don't, Mother, don't.

ZINIDA

Count, you drew in advance, I have it written down,
eighty francs and twenty centimes. Will you pay this
money, too?

MANCINI

Certainly, certainly. You will get three thousand
and one hundred. [*Laughing*] Twenty centimes!
I never thought I could be so accurate. [*Seriously*]
Yes, my friends. My daughter Consuelo—the Countess—and the Baron, expressed their desire to bid
farewell to the whole cast.

HE

The Baron, too?

MANCINI

Yes, Auguste, too. They want to do it during the intermission. Therefore, I ask you to gather here . . the more decent ones . . . but please don't make it too crowded! HE, will you, sir, be kind enough to run into the buffet and tell them to bring right away a basket of champagne, bottles and glasses—you understand?

HE

Yes, Count.

MANCINI

Wait a minute, what's the hurry—what is this, a new costume? You are all burning like the devils in hell!

HE

You do me too much honour, Count, I am not a devil. I am merely a poor sinner who the devils are frying a little. [*He goes out, bowing like a clown.*]

MANCINI

A gifted chap, but too cunning.

Briquet

It's the Tango colour, in honour of your daughter, Count. He needs it for a new stunt, which he doesn't want to tell in advance. Don't you want to sit down, Count?

Mancini

Auguste is waiting for me, but . . . it's all right. [*Takes a seat.*] Nevertheless I am sorry to leave you, my friend. High society, certainly, prerogatives of the title, castles of exalted noblemen, but where could I find such freedom, and . . . such simplicity. . . . And besides, these announcements, these burning posters, which take your breath in the morning, they had something which summoned, which encouraged. . . . *There*, my friends, I shall become old.

Briquet

But pleasures of a higher kind, Count. Why are you silent, Zinida?

Zinida

I'm listening.

Mancini

By the way, my dear, how do you like my suit?

You have wonderful taste. [*Spreads out his lace tie and lace cuffs.*]

ZINIDA

I like it. You look like a nobleman of the courts of long ago.

MANCINI

Yes? But don't you think it is too conspicuous? Who wears lace and satin now? This dirty democracy will soon make us dress ourselves in sack cloth. [*With a sigh*] Auguste told me that this jabot was out of place.

ZINIDA

The Baron is too severe.

MANCINI

Yes, but it seems to me he is right. I am a little infected with your fancy. [*HE returns. Two waiters follow him, carrying a basket of champagne and glasses. They prepare everything on the table.*]

MANCINI

Ah! *merci*, HE. But, please, none of this bourgeoise exploding of corks; be slower and more modest. Send the bill to Baron Regnard. Then, we will be here, Briquet. I must go.

ZINIDA

[*Looks at her watch*]: Yes, the act is going to end soon.

MANCINI

Heavens! [*Disappears in a hurry.*]

BRIQUET

The devil take him!

ZINIDA

[*Pointing to the waiter*]: Not so loud, Louis!

BRIQUET

No! The devil take him! And why couldn't you help me, Mother? You left me alone to talk to him. High Society! High pleasures! Swindler! [*HE and* ZINIDA *laugh. The waiters smile.*]

BRIQUET

[*To the waiters*]: What are you laughing about? You can go. We will help ourselves. Whiskey and soda, Jean! [*In a low and angry voice*] Champagne! [*Enter* JACKSON, *in his clown's costume.*]

JACKSON

A whiskey and soda for me, too! At least I hear
some laughter here. Those idiots have simply forgotten how to laugh. My sun was rising and setting
and crawling all over the ring——and not a smile!
Look at my bottom, shines like a mirror! [*Turns
around quickly.*] Beg your pardon, Zinida. And
you don't look badly to-night, HE. Look out for
your cheeks. I hate beauties.

BRIQUET

A benefit performance crowd!

JACKSON

[*Looking in a hand mirror, correcting his make-
up*]: In the orchestra there are some Barons and
Egyptian mummies. I got a belly-ache from fright.
I am an honest clown. I can't stand it when they
look at me as if I had stolen a handkerchief. HE,
please give them a good many slaps to-night.

HE

Be quiet, Jim. I shall avenge you. [*He goes out.*]

ZINIDA

And how is Bezano?

JACKSON

[*Grumbling*]: Bezano! A crazy success. But he is crazy, he will break his neck to-morrow. Why does he run such a risk? Or perhaps he has wings, like a god? Devil take it. It's disgusting to look at him. It's not work any more.

BRIQUET

You are right, Jim! It is not work any more. To your health, old comrade, Jackson.

JACKSON

To yours, Louis.

BRIQUET

It is not work any more, since these Barons came here! Do you hear? They are laughing. But I am indignant, I am indignant, Jim! What do they want here, these Barons? Let them steal hens in other hen roosts, and leave us in peace. Ah! Had I been Secretary of the Interior, I should have made an iron fence between us and those people.

JACKSON

I am very sorry myself for our dear little Consuelo I don't know why, but it seems to me that we

all look to-day more like swindlers than honest artists. Don't you think so, Zinida?

ZINIDA

Everybody does what he wants. It's Consuelo's
business and her father's.

BRIQUET

No, Mother, that's not true! Not everybody does
what he wants, but it turns out this way . . . devil
knows why.

[*Enter* ANGELICA *and* THOMAS, *an athlete.*]

ANGELICA

Is this where we're going to have champagne?

BRIQUET

And you're glad already?

THOMAS

There it is! Oh, oh, what a lot!

ANGELICA

The Count told me to come here. I met him.

BRIQUET

[*Angrily*]: All right, if he said so, but there is no reason to enjoy it. Look out, Angelica, you will have a bad end. I see you through and through. How does she work, Thomas?

THOMAS

Very well.

ANGELICA

[*In a low voice*]: How angry Papa Briquet is to-night.
[*Enter HE, TILLY, POLLY, and other actors, all in their costumes.*]

TILLY

Do you really want champagne?

POLLY

I don't want it at all. Do you, Tilly?

TILLY

And I don't want it. HE, did you see how the Count walks? [*Walks, imitating MANCINI. Laughter.*]

Polly

Let me be the Baron. Take my arm. Look out, ass, you stepped on my beloved family tree!

Angelica

It'll soon be finished. Consuelo is galloping now. It is her waltz. What a success she is having!

[*All listen to the waltz.* Tilly *and* Polly *are singing it softly.*]

Angelica

She is so beautiful! Are those her flowers?

[*They listen. Suddenly, a crash as if a broken wall were tumbling down; applause, shouting, screaming; much motion on the stage. The actors are pouring champagne. New ones come in, talking and laughing. When they notice the director and the champagne, they become quiet and modest.*]

Voices

They're coming! What a success! I should say, since all the orchestra seats . . . And what will it be when they see the Tango? Don't be envious, Alphonse.

BRIQUET

Silence! Not so much noise, please! Zinida, look here, don't be so quiet! High society!

[*Enter* CONSUELO, *on the arm of the* BARON *who is stiff and erect. She is happy.* MANCINI, *serious and happy. Behind them, riders, actors, actresses. The* BARON *has in his button-hole a fiery-red rose. All applaud and cry:* "*Bravo, bravo!*"]

CONSUELO

Friends . . . my dears . . . Father, I can't . . . [*Throws herself into* MANCINI'S *arms, and hides her face on his shoulders.* MANCINI *looks with a smile over her head at the* BARON. BARON *smiles slightly, but remains earnest and motionless. A new burst of applause.*]

BRIQUET

Enough, children! Enough!

MANCINI

Calm yourself, calm yourself, my child. How they all love you! [*Taking a step forward*] Ladies and gentlemen, Baron Regnard did me the honour yesterday, to ask for the hand of my daughter, the

Countess Veronica, whom you knew under the name of Consuelo. Please take your glasses.

CONSUELO

No, I am still Consuelo, to-night, and I shall always be Consuelo! Zinida, dear! [*Falls on the neck of* ZINIDA. *Fresh applause.*]

BRIQUET

Stop it! Silence! Take your glasses. What are you standing here for? If you came, then take the glasses.

TILLY

[*Trembling*]: They are frightened. You take yours first, Papa, and we will follow.
[*They take the glasses.* CONSUELO *is near the* BARON, *holding the sleeve of his dress coat with her left hand. In her right hand, she has a glass of champagne, which spills over.*]

BARON

You are spilling your wine, Consuelo.

CONSUELO

Ah! It is nothing! I am frightened, too. Are you, Father?

MANCINI

Silly child. [*An awkward silence.*]

BRIQUET

[*With a step forward*]: Countess! As the director of the circus, who was happy enough . . . to
witness . . . many times . . . your successes . . .

CONSUELO

I do not *like* this, Papa Briquet! I am Consuelo.
What do you want to do with me? I shall cry. I
don't want this "Countess." Give me a kiss, Briquet!

BRIQUET

Ah, Consuelo! Books have killed you.

[*Kisses her with tears. Laughter, applause. The
clowns cluck like hens, bark, and express their
emotions in many other ways. The motley
crowd of clowns, which is ready for the panto-
mime, becomes more and more lively. The
BARON is motionless, there is a wide space
around him; the people touch glasses with him
in a hurry, and go off to one side. With* CON-
SUELO *they clink willingly and cheerfully. She
kisses the women.*]

Jackson

Silence! Consuelo, from to-day on, I extinguish
my sun. Let the dark night come after you leave us.
You were a nice comrade and worker, we all loved
you and will love the traces of your little feet on the
sand. Nothing remains to us!

Consuelo

You are so good, so good, Jim. So good that
there is no one better. And your sun is better than
all the other suns. I laughed so much at it. Alfred,
dear, why don't you come? I was looking for you.

Bezano

My congratulations, Countess.

Consuelo

Alfred, I am Consuelo!

Bezano

When you are on horseback; but here—I congratulate you, Countess. [*He passes, only slightly
touching* Consuelo's *glass.* Consuelo *still holds it.*
Mancini *looks at the* Baron *with a smile. The latter is motionless.*]

BRIQUET

Nonsense, Bezano. You are making Consuelo unhappy. She is a good comrade.

CONSUELO

No, it's all right.

ANGELICA

You'll dance the Tango with her to-night, so how
is she a countess?

TILLY

May I clink glasses with you, Consuelo? You
know Polly has died of grief already, and I am
going to die. I have such a weak stomach.
[*Laughter;* BARON *shows slight displeasure. General
motion.*]

MANCINI

Enough, enough! The intermission is over.

CONSUELO

Already? It's so nice here.

BRIQUET

I shall prolong it. They can wait. Tell them,
Thomas.

Mancini

Auguste, the musicians of the orchestra, too, ask permission to congratulate you and Consuelo. Do you . . . ?

Baron

Certainly, certainly.

[*Enter crowd of musicians. The conductor, an old Italian, lifts his glass solemnly and without looking at the* Baron.]

The Conductor

Consuelo! They call you Countess here, but for me you were and are *Consuelo*.

Consuelo

Certainly!

The Conductor

Consuelo! My violins and bassoons, my trumpets and drums, all are drinking your health. Be happy, dear child, as you were happy here. And we shall conserve for ever in our hearts the fair memory of our light-winged fairy, who guided our bows so long. I have finished! Give my love to our beautiful Italy, Consuelo.

[Applause, compliments. The musicians one after another clink glasses and go out into the corridor. CONSUELO is almost crying.]

MANCINI

Don't be so sensitive, my child, it is indecent. Had I known that you would respond this way to this comedy—Auguste, look how touched this little heart is!

BARON

Calm yourself, Consuelo.

CONSUELO

It is all right. Ah, Father, listen!

[The musicians are playing the Tango in the corridor. Exclamations.]

MANCINI

You see. It is for you.

CONSUELO

They are so nice. My Tango! I want to dance. Who is going to dance with me? *[Looks around, seeking BEZANO, who turns away sadly.]* Who, then?

Voices

Baron! Let the Baron dance! Baron!

Baron

All right. [*Takes* Consuelo's *arm, and stands in the centre of a circle which is formed.*] I do not know how to dance the Tango, but I shall hold tight. Dance, Consuelo. [*He stands with legs spread, heavily and awkwardly, like an iron-moulded man, holding* Consuelo's *arm firmly and seriously.*]

Mancini

[*Applauding*]: Bravo! Bravo! [Consuelo *makes a few restless movements, and pulls her arm away.*]

Consuelo

No, I can't this way. How stupid! Let me go! [*She goes to* Zinida *and embraces her, as if hiding herself. The music still plays. The* Baron *goes off quietly to the side. There is an unfriendly silence among the cast. They shrug their shoulders.*]

Mancini

[*Alone*]: Bravo! Bravo! It is charming, it is exquisite!

JACKSON

Not entirely, Count.

[TILLY *and* POLLY *imitate the* BARON *and* CONSUELO
without moving from their places.]

TILLY

[*Shrieking*]: Let me go!

POLLY

No, I'll not.   Dance!

[*The music stops abruptly.   General, too loud
laughter; the clowns bark and roar.   Papa
BRIQUET gesticulates, in order to re-establish
silence.   The BARON is apparently as indifferent as before.*]

MANCINI

Really these vagabonds are becoming too imperti-
nent. [*Shrugging his shoulders*] It smells of the
stable. You cannot help it, Auguste!

BARON

Don't be upset, Count.

HE

[*Holding his glass, approaches the* BARON]: Baron
Will you permit me to make a toast?

BARON

Make it.

HE

To your dance! [*Slight laughter in the crowd.*]

BARON

I don't dance!

HE

Then another one, Baron. Let us drink to those who know how to wait longer, until they get it.

BARON

I do not accept any toasts which I do not understand. Say it more simply.

[*Voice of a woman: "Bravo, HE!" Slight laughter.*

MANCINI *says something hastily to* BRIQUET; *the latter spreads his arms in gesture of helplessness.* JACKSON *takes HE by the arm.*]

JACKSON

Beat it, HE! The Baron doesn't like jokes.

HE

But I want to drink with the Baron. What can be simpler? Simpler? Baron, let us drink to the very small distance which will always remain 'twixt the cup and the lip! [*Spills his wine, and laughs.*] [*The* BARON *turns his back on him, indifferently. The music plays in the ring. The bell rings.*]

BRIQUET

[*Relieved*]: There! To the ring, ladies and gentlemen, to the ring, to the ring!
[*The actresses run out. The crowd becomes smaller; laughter and voices.*]

MANCINI

[*Much excited, whispers to the* BARON]: "Auguste, Auguste——"

BRIQUET

[*To* ZINIDA]: Thank heaven they're beginning. Ah, Mother, I asked you . . . but you want a scandal by all means, and you always——

ZINIDA

Let me alone, Louis.
[*HE approaches Consuelo, who is alone.*]

CONSUELO

HE, deary, how are you?   I thought you didn't want even to come near me.   [*In a low voice*] Did you notice Bezano?

HE

I was waiting for my turn, Queen.   It was so difficult to get through the crowd to approach you.

CONSUELO

Through the crowd?   [*With a sad smile*]   I am quite alone.   What do you want, Father?

MANCINI

Child! Auguste . . .

CONSUELO

[*Pulling away her hand*]:   Let me alone!   I'll soon be— Come here, HE.   What did you say to him?   They all laughed.   I couldn't understand. What?

HE

I joked, Consuelo.

CONSUELO

Please don't, HE, don't make him angry; he is so

terrible. Did you see how he pressed my arm? I
wanted to scream. [*With tears in her eyes*] He
hurt me!

HE

It's not too late yet. Refuse him.

CONSUELO

It *is* too late, HE. Don't talk about it.

HE

Do you want it? I will take you away from here.

CONSUELO

Where to? [*Laughs.*] Ah, my dear little silly
boy, where could you take me to. All right, be quiet.
How pale you are! You too, love me? Don't HE,
please don't! Why do they all love me?

HE

You are so beautiful!

CONSUELO

No, no. It's not true. They must not love me.
I was still a little cheerful, but when they began to
speak . . . so nicely . . . and about Italy . . .

and to bid farewell, as if I were dying, I thought I should begin to cry. Don't talk, don't talk, but drink to . . . my happiness. [*With a sad smile*] To my happiness, HE. What are you doing?

HE

I am throwing away the glass from which you drank with the others. I shall give you another one. Wait a minute. [*Goes to pour champagne. CONSUELO walks about thoughtfully. Almost all are gone. Only the principal figures are left.*]

MANCINI

[*Coming to her*]: But it is really becoming indecent, Veronica. Auguste is so nice, he is waiting for you, and you talk here with this clown. Some stupid secrets. They're looking at you—it is becoming noticeable. It is high time, Veronica, to get rid of these habits.

CONSUELO

[*Loudly*]: Let me alone, Father! I want to do so, and will do so. They are all my friends. Do you hear? Let me alone!

BARON

Don't, Count. Please, Consuelo, talk to whomever you please and as much as you want. Would you like a cigar, Count? Dear Briquet, please order them to prolong the intermission a little more.

BRIQUET

With pleasure, Baron. The orchestra crowd can be a little angry. [*Goes, and returns shortly. HE gives a glass to* CONSUELO.]

HE

Here is your glass. To your happiness, to your freedom, Consuelo!

CONSUELO

And where is yours? We must touch our glasses.

HE

You leave half.

CONSUELO

Must I drink so much? HE, deary, I shall become drunk. I still have to ride.

HE

No, you will not be drunk. Dear little girl, did you forget that I am your magician? Be quiet and

drink. I charmed the wine. My witchery is in it.
Drink, goddess.

Consuelo

[*Lingeringly*]: What kind eyes you have. But
why are you so pale?

He

Because I love you. Look at my kind eyes and
drink; give yourself up to my charms, goddess! You
shall fall asleep, and wake again, as before. Do you
remember? And you shall see your country, your
sky . . .

Consuelo

[*Bringing the glass to her lips*]: I shall see all
this; is that true?

He

[*Growing paler*]: Yes! Awake, goddess, and remember the time when, covered with snow-white sea-
foam, thou didst emerge from the sky blue waters.
Remember heaven, and the low eastern wind, and the
whisper of the foam at thy marble feet. . . .

Consuelo

[*Drinking*]: There! Look! Just a half! Take

it. But what is the matter with you? Are you laughing or crying?

HE

I am laughing and crying.

MANCINI

[*Pushing HE away, slightly*]: Enough, Countess, my patience is exhausted. If Auguste is good enough to allow it, then I, your Father—Your arm, Countess! Will you step aside, sir?

CONSUELO

I am tired.

MANCINI

You are not too tired to chatter and drink wine with a clown, and when your duty calls you—Briquet! Tell them to ring the bell. It is time.

CONSUELO

I am tired, Father.

ZINIDA

Count, it is cruel. Don't you see how pale she has become?

Baron

What is the matter with you, dear little Consuelo?

Consuelo

Nothing.

Zinida

She simply needs a rest, Baron. She hasn't sat down yet . . . and so much excitement. . . . Sit down here, dear child. Cover yourself and rest a little. Men are so cruel!

Consuelo

I still have to work. [*Closing her eyes.*] And the roses, are they ready?

Zinida

Ready, dear, ready. You will have such an extraordinary carpet. You will gallop as if on air. Rest.

Polly

Do you want some moosic? We will play you a song; do you want it?

Consuelo

[*Smiling, eyes closed*]: Yes, I do.

[*The clowns play a soft and näive song: tilly-polly, tilly-polly. General silence. HE sits in the corner with his face turned away. JACKSON watches him out of the corner of his eye, and drinks wine, lazily. The BARON, in his usual pose, wide and heavily spread legs, looks at the pale face of CONSUELO, with his bulging motionless eyes.*]

Consuelo

[*With a sudden cry*]: Ah! Pain!

Zinida

What is it, Consuelo?

Mancini

My child! Are you sick! Calm yourself.

Baron

[*Growing pale*]: Wait a moment. . . . She was too much excited. . . . Consuelo!

Consuelo

[*Gets up, looking before her with wide-open eyes, as if she were listening to something within herself*]:

Ah! I feel pain. Here at the heart. Father, what
is it? I am afraid. What is it? My feet too . . .
I can't stand. . . . [*Falls on divan, her eyes wide
open.*]

MANCINI

[*Running about*]: Bring a doctor! Heavens, it is
terrible! Auguste, Baron . . . It never happened to her. It is nerves, nerves. . . . Calm
yourself, calm, child——

BRIQUET

Bring a doctor! [*Somebody runs for a doctor.*]

JACKSON

[*In a voice full of fear*]: HE, what is the matter
with you?

HE

It is death, Consuelo, my little Queen. I killed you.
You are dying.
[*He cries, loudly and bitterly. CONSUELO with a
scream, closes her eyes, and becomes silent and
quiet. All are in terrible agitation. The BARON
is motionless, and sees only CONSUELO.*]

MANCINI

[*Furious*]: You are lying, rascal! Damned clown! What did you give her? You poisoned her! Murderer! Bring a doctor!

HE

A doctor will not help. You are dying, my little Queen. Consuelo! Consuelo!
[BEZANO *rushes in, cries:* "BRIQUET!" *becomes silent and looks with horror at* CONSUELO. *Somebody else come in.* BRIQUET *is making gestures for someone to close the door*].

CONSUELO

[*In a dull and distant voice*]: You are joking, HE? Don't frighten me. I am so frightened. Is that death? I don't want it. Ah, HE, my darling HE, tell me that you are joking, I am afraid, my dear, golden HE!
[HE *pushes away the* BARON, *with a commanding gesture, and stands in his place near* CONSUELO. *The* BARON *stands as before, seeing only* CONSUELO.]

HE

Yes, I am joking. Don't you hear how I laugh, Consuelo? They all laugh at you here, my silly child.

Don't laugh, Jim. She is tired, and wants to sleep.
How can you laugh, Jim! Sleep my dear, sleep my
heart, sleep my love.

CONSUELO

Yes, I have no more pain. Why did you joke that
way, and frighten me? Now I laugh at myself. You
told me, didn't you, that I . . . should . . .
live . . . eternally?

HE

Yes, Consuelo! You shall live eternally. Sleep. Be
calm. [*Lifts up his arms, as if straining with all his
forces to lift her soul higher.*] How easy it is now!
How much light, how many lights are burning about
you. . . . The light is blinding you.

CONSUELO

Yes, light . . . Is that the ring?

HE

No, it is the sea and the sun . . . what a sun!
Don't you feel that you are the foam, white sea-foam,
and you are flying to the sun? You feel light, you
have no body, you are flying higher, my love!

I am flying. I am the sea-foam, and this is the
sun, it shines . . . so strong. . . . I feel
well.

[*She dies.   Silence.   HE stays a moment with lifted
arms, then takes a long look, lets his arms fall,
and shakingly goes off to one side.   He stands
still for a moment, then sits down, drops his head
on his hands, and struggles lonesomely with the
torpidity of coming death.*]

BRIQUET

[*Slowly*] :   She has fallen asleep, Mother?

ZINIDA

[*Dropping the dead hand*] :   I am afraid not.   . . .
Step aside, Louis.   Baron, it is better for you to step
aside.   Baron!   Do you hear me?   [*Weeps.*]   She is
dead, Louis.

[*The clowns and* BRIQUET *are crying.*   MANCINI *is
overwhelmed.   The* BARON *and* HE *are motionless, each in his place.*]

JACKSON

[*Drawing out a large prismatic clown's handkerchief to wipe away his tears*] :   Faded, like a flower.
Sleep, little Consuelo!   The only thing that remains
of you is the trace of your little feet on the sand.
[*Cries.*]   Ah, what did you do, what did you do, HE!
. . .   It would have been better if you had never
come to us.

[*There is music in the ring.*]

Briquet

[*Gesticulating*]: The music! Stop the music! They are crazy there. What a misfortune!

[*Someone runs off. Zinida approaches the crying Bezano and strokes his bowed, pomaded head. When he notices her, he catches her hand and presses it to his eyes. The Baron takes the rose from his button-hole, tears off the petals, and drops it, grinding it with his foot. A few pale faces peer through the door, the same masquerade crowd.*]

Zinida

[*Over the head of Bezano*]: Louis, we must call the police.

Mancini

[*Awakening from his stupor, screams*]: The police! Call the police! It's a murder! I am Count Mancini, I am Count Mancini! They will cut off your head, murderer, damned clown, thief! I myself will kill you, rascal! Ah, you! [*HE lifts his heavy head with difficulty.*]

He

They will cut off my head? And what **more** . . . Your Excellency?

BARON

Sir! Listen, sir! I am going for the police. Stop
it, sir. [*He suddenly takes a step forward, and looking HE in the eyes, speaks in a hoarse voice, with a
cough, holding one hand at his throat.*] I am the
witness. I saw. I am a witness. I saw how he put
poison . . . I——

[*He leaves the room, suddenly, with the same straight,
heavy steps. All move away from him, frightened. HE drops his head again. From time to
time a tremor shakes his body.*]

JACKSON

[*Clasping his hands*]: Then it is all true? Poisoned! What a vile man you are, HE. Is this the
way to play? Now wait for the last slap of the exe-
cutioner! [*Makes the gesture around his neck, of the
guillotine. Tilly and Polly repeat the gesture.*]

ZINIDA

Leave his soul alone, Jim. He was a man, and he
loved. Happy Consuelo!

[*A shot is heard in the corridor. THOMAS, frightened,
runs in and points to his head.*]

Thomas

Baron . . . Baron . . . his head . . .
He shot himself? . . .

Briquet

[*Throwing his arms up*]: God! What is it? The
Baron? What a calamity for our circus.

Mancini

The Baron? The Baron? No. What are you
standing here for? Ah!

Briquet

Calm down, Count. Who would have believed it?
Such a respectable . . . gentleman!

He

[*Lifting his head with difficulty; he sees only dimly
with his dulled eyes*]: What more? What happened?

Thomas

The Baron shot himself. Honestly. Straight here!
He's lying out yonder.

HE

[*Thinking it over*]: Baron? [*Laughs.*] Then the Baron burst?

JACKSON

Stop it! It's shameless. A man died and you . . . What's the matter with you, HE?

HE

[*Stands up, lifted to his feet by the last gleam of consciousness and life, speaks strongly and indignantly*]: You loved her so much, Baron? So much? My Consuelo? And you want to be ahead of me even *there?* No! I am coming. We shall prove then whose she is to be for ever. . . .
[*He catches at his throat, falls on his back. People run to him. General agitation.*]

CURTAIN

PAPA IS ALL

Comedy. 3 acts. By Patterson Greene. 3 males, 3 females. Interior. Modern costumes.

Papa Is All, first produced at the Guild Theatre in New York, is a cheerful comedy about the Pennsylvania Dutch. Papa is a tyrant, club-footed, ugly tempered. Emma, the daughter, is in love with a surveyor who wants to marry her. The son, Jake, wants to simplify farm life by the installation of machinery. Mama is wistful for the friendly association with neighbors that is a normal part of even the most orthodox Mennonite life. Emma precipitates a crises by stealing away to attend a picture show in Lancaster in the company of her young surveyor. A neighbor inadvertently reveals Emma's secret, and Papa sweeps off in a rage to shoot the pleasant young man. Apparently the gods are on the family's side. The car in which Papa is riding to his shooting is fortunately wrecked at a railroad crossing and Pappa happily disappears. What his fate is, and how finally Papa is really done in, unfolds in the third act. "A light and completely entertaining play . . . popular comedy with a funny plot and a background of Mennonite manners . . . well-bred lark in folksy style."—*New York Times.* Excellent comedy for Little Theatres and colleges.

(Royalty, $35.00.)

NO TIME FOR COMEDY

Comedy. 3 acts. By S. N. Behrman. 4 males, 3 females. 2 interiors. Modern costumes.

First produced by Katharine Cornell and the Playwright's Company in New York with Katharine Cornell and Laurence Olivier in the leading roles. Gaylord Easterbrook is a clever young playwright whose comedies are highly successful. He is married to Linda, a brilliant actress who stars in all his plays. But Gay is discontented and restless, and he feels that the modern tempo and constant change demand reality and a serious approach. He is encouraged in this opinion by Amanda Smith, a restless dabbler and society woman. With her as an inspiration Gay manages to write a serious play about death and the Spanish Loyalists. Through all this apparent affair Linda carefully walks, and of course, comes out the undisputed winner when it is obvious that Gay is not going to elope with Amanda, who wants to run away. "Another 'must' on the play-going curriculum."— N. Y. *Journal-American. "No Time For Comedy* is a dainty, amusing delight."—N. Y. *Times.*

(Royalty, $35.00.)